THE JAPANESE ECONOMY AND THE AMERICAN BUSINESSMAN

Daniel Metraux

Mellen Studies in Business
Volume 5

The Edwin Mellen Press
Lewiston/Queenston/Lampeter

Library of Congress Cataloging-in-Publication Data

The Japanese Economy and The American Businessman
/ by Daniel Metraux.
   p. cm. -- (Mellen studies in business : v. 5)
   Bibliography: p.
   Includes index.
   ISBN 0-88946-158-9
   1. Japan--Economic conditions. 2. Japan--Commerce. 3. Japan-
-Politics and government. 4. Japan--Commerce--United States.
5. United States--Commerce--Japan. I. Title. II. Series: Mellen
studies in business ; vol. 5.
HC462.M454 1989
382' .0952073--dc20   89-9404
                                                           CIP

This is volume 5 in the continuing series
Mellen Studies in Business
Volume 5 ISBN 0-88946-158-9
MSB Series ISBN 0-88946-152-X

A CIP catalog record for this book
is available from the British Library.

The Edwin Mellen Press   The Edwin Mellen Press
Box 450   Box 67
Lewiston, NY   Queenston, Ontario
USA 14092   CANADA L0S 1L0

The Edwin Mellen Press, Ltd.
Lampeter, Dyfed, Wales,
UNITED KINGDOM SA48 7DY

Printed in the United States of America

TABLE OF CONTENTS

Preface   v

Introduction   vii

Chapter I
Why Has Japan Been So Successful?   1

Chapter II
Communicating With The Japanese   31

Chapter III
The Culture of Japanese Management   51

Chapter IV
*The Changing Nature of the Occupational Structure
of The Japanese Economy*   69

Chapter V
Government and Business   83

Chapter VI
U.S.-Japanese Economic Relations in the 1980s   101

Chapter VII
Trading and Marketing With The Japanese   129

Chapter VIII
Technology and The Future   155

Source Materials/Bibliography   163

Index   169

PREFACE

There are many books in print that deal with various aspects of business life in Japan. They range from popular works such as *Theory Z* to some very technical works on the Japanese economy. There are, however, few if any current texts that deal with the whole dimension of the Japanese economy written for the college student taking a class on Japanese business. After trying in vain to find readings for my own class on Japanese Business History, I researched and wrote this text for class use. Hopefully this work will be of use to other students elsewhere, to businessmen who want to do business in Japan, and to others interested in Japan's economy.

I wish to acknowledge the help of Richard Rice, Lucien Ellington, Gordon Hammock, Vicky Nolton and others who read all or part of this text and made useful comments. I wish to thank Mary Baldwin College for its support, Beverly Askegaard for her careful editing, and Sandy Sprouse for her typing and other work. Finally, I wish to thank my wife, Judy, and my children, Katie and David, for their tolerance and love throughout this lengthy project.

Daniel A. Metraux
Staunton, Virginia
January 1989

INTRODUCTION

Every day Americans are bombarded with a seemingly endless series of news stories describing the red ink in U.S. balance of payments, the growing gap in the trade balance with Japan, and floundering attempts by the Reagan Administration to address these crises. Both the Reagan Administration and many members of Congress perceive the continued economic success of Japan as a genuine threat to the American economy. They are bothered by the fact that while the U.S. balance of trade has worsened in recent years, Japanese businesses have flourished in world markets. Sadly, these developments are bringing out some of the worst aspects of American jingoism and are causing many Japanese to question their commitments to the United States. The nearly 60 billion dollar trade deficit with Japan in 1986 has brought forth many unfair and unattractive characterizations of Japanese behavior and policies. Many Americans are blaming Japan for their own economic woes and frustrations rather than looking for intelligent solutions domestically.

Some American politicians like Congressman Gephardt of Missouri feel that the United States can and should punish Japan for taking advantage of American economic weaknesses. They demand that it is up to Japan to make all the concessions, but what they fail to realize is that the Japanese now have the power to retaliate in such a way as to send the U.S. economy into a deep depression.

Today Americans are using Japanese money to finance their growing budget deficits. Forty percent of the Treasury Bonds sold at auctions in the late 1980s were bought by Japanese corporations and the Japanese are pouring billions of dollars into the U.S. stock market. If the Japanese should decide to stop buying these bonds, American interest rates would skyrocket and Wall Street would be seriously affected by a Japanese boycott or sellout.

Despite the very real possibility of Japanese retaliation, however, some Americans persist in actions that can only make the crisis more serious. Take, for example, the 1987 Gephardt Amendment in the House of Representatives that was vetoed by President Reagan. This act is heavily protectionist and would exact substantial penalties on the Japanese if they refused to give in to American demands. This bill is reminiscent of the Hawley-Smoot Act of 1930. Just before Congress passed this disastrous act, which helped to plunge the world into an era of vicious trade wars and growing depressions, Representative Willis C. Hawley said:

> If this bill is enacted into law...we will have a renewed era of prosperity which will increase our wealth, our employment, our comfort, promote our trade abroad, and will keep the United States before the world as the premier nation of solid finance.

Like the Hawley-Smoot Act, the Gephart Amendment could be very detrimental. Are Americans too naive to realize that piecemeal measures to reduce the trade deficit with Japan will not have far-ranging multi-lateral consequences? Such initiatives aimed at bilateral trade not only violate some basic trade rules that the U.S. spelled out for the world a while ago, but they could also easily backfire with Japanese retaliation. They also ignore the reality of our trade relationship with Japan.

Japan depends heavily on the export of manufactured goods to finance the import of raw materials from OPEC nations, the Third World, the U.S. and Australia. American export strength depends greatly on the export of agricultural products to European and developing nation markets. This means that even if the United States were to balance trade, it would still have a deficit with Japan. Japan-bashing will only aggravate our trade problems.

Clearly, closer cooperation between the United States and Japan is essential. The two economies are so deeply intertwined that any major disruption would have serious consequences for both sides. This is especially true in the late 1980s as Japan is making the painful shift from an economy based on manufacturing to a post-industrial economy based on service and information industries.

The major obstacle to such cooperation is the almost total lack of understanding Americans have of Japan, together with a certain resistance to achieving better communication and cooperation. The real deficit with Japan is not measurable in billions of dollars of imports minus exports. Nor is it just the much-publicized gap in productivity growth rates, or the gap in research and development spending. It is, first and foremost, an attitudinal gap, an awareness gap, a deficit in cross-cultural communication skills.

The purpose of this work is to analyze the various aspects of Japanese history, society, politics, business life, and relations with the United States to give Americans a clearer view of their major economic partner. This is not a complete view -- Japan's important relations with China and the rest of Asia, Europe, and the Soviet Union are only mentioned in passing. One hopes that the reader of this work will come away with a better understanding of the factors that have led to Japan's successes and problems, as well as the nature of its unique system of management and close business-government cooperation. A secondary goal is to provide some discussion on Japanese-American relations and information on how Americans might better communicate with the Japanese and more successfully market their goods in Japan.

Daniel Metraux
Greensboro, Vermont
Summer, 1987

CHAPTER I

WHY HAS JAPAN BEEN SO SUCCESSFUL?

To date Japan is alone among the Third World nations with the capacity to compete on an equal basis with the great nations of the West. Japan's success is hardly new. A hundred and fifty years ago Japan had little of the technology of the West and made no attempt to resist the first concerted efforts to the United States to open Nippon to the outside world. By the 1890s Japan was already a powerful military and industrial power, and by 1905 it had signed a naval treaty with the British and had defeated the Russian army and navy in a brief but furious war. By the early 1940s the Japanese had a huge empire stretching across much of East Asia and was holding its own in a massive war against the United States across the Pacific. Japan was eventually crushed in the Pacific War and had to endure seven years of American military occupation (1945-52), but Japan's recovery after the 1950s is legendary.

Today Japan is one of the wealthiest nations on earth. For example, in 1986 the average income of the 121 million Japanese surpassed that of the 242 million Americans: $17,000 as compared with $16,000.[1] Salaried workers in Tokyo fared even better in 1986. They earned 5.51 million yen ($44,080) a year and held tangible property worth an average of 23.57 million yen ($188,560).[2] It is important to note, however, that the cost of many commodities is higher in Japan than in the United States.[3] According to one recent estimate, for example, the average Japanese family in the mid-1980s spent a third more money per month to buy food than a family in the United States.[4] Housing costs are also clearly higher in Japan than in the United States. Thus, while income is higher in Japan, it is difficult to compare the quality of life in the United States and Japan.

Today, Japan is very successful, but there is also evidence on the horizon of a certain degree of economic decline that Japan's great growth cannot continue and that the Japanese will soon have to cope with some of the problems that come with economic maturity.

Geography, Population and Resources:

The Japanese have had to work hard to overcome some severe disadvantages, such as a lack of natural resources and a lack of arable land. However, one can plausibly argue that the necessity of struggling to meet adversity is partially responsible for this success story.

Japan is not a small country by European standards. It is considerably larger than Italy and half again as big as Great Britain. Its huge population, however, must live in tightly confined areas because Japan consists of a mass of sharp mountains broken up by a narrow flat coastline, narrow valleys, and a few larger plains, including the Kanto Plain around Tokyo and the Kansai region that includes Osaka and Kyoto.

Japan is an island nation short of everything except people. In 1987 it had a population (121 million) half as large as that of the United States (242 million) in an area smaller than California. But Japan seems even more crowded than those numbers would suggest because the mountains take up two-thirds of the land area and the farmers take up almost half of what isleft. Japan's land area is 378,000 square kilometers or about 151,000 square miles. Of that, 66.9 percent is mountains and forest, and another 3.1 percent is rivers and channels. Farmland takes up 14.3 percent, leaving houses, factories, roads, parks, schools, and stores to be squeezed into the remaining 15.7 percent.[5]

Japan has a very stable population. Its birth rate in 1986 dropped to its lowest level since 1899, and the 1.38 million babies born during 1987 represented the second lowest figure in the previous 20 years. The 1986 death rate of 750,000 dropped by 2,000 from 1985; cancer deaths (190,000 plus) and suicides (25,659) set record highs, but the death rate among infants (5.3 per 1,000) was the lowest in the world. Marriage rates for 1986 reached a new low (5.9 per 1000).[6] Japanese women now live an average of 80 years with Japanese men not very far behind. Thus, the average age of Japanese men is rising rapidly. By the start of the next century Japan may well have the oldest population of any major industrial nation with a small number of young workers obliged to support a large number of retired people. This may provoke a massive economic, political, and social crisis that will confront the Japanese in the next few years.

The Japanese are further troubled by the lack of most essential resources. There is no oil, few worthwhile minerals, and little coal. Much of Japan's food must be purchased abroad. One wag once pointed out with a certain degree of veracity that the only foods produced in abundance by Japan are tangerines and rice. Except for some fruits and green vegetables, Japan must import vast amounts of other foodstuffs including soy and grain.

There are, however, some natural advantages. There is ample rain throughout the year; only rarely does Japan suffer from drought. Rushing streams produce a large amount of waterpower. Japan's climate, which is easily comparable with that of the east coast of the United States, is good for food production. Hokkaido, the northernmost of the four large islands of Japan, approximates New England and southern Quebec. Tokyo's climate is very similar to that of Washington, D.C. while the bulk of Japan's population, which is located between Tokyo and Osaka, lives at the same latitude as North Carolina. The lower reaches of Kyushu, the southern-most island, are at the same latitude as southern Alabama and Louisiana. Rain and a seasonable climate permit the Japanese to make maximum use of their land for agricultural purposes and provide for good natural living conditions despite frequent typhoons and earthquakes.

Historical and Cultural Factors:

It is the cultural fabric of the Japanese people that has contributed most to their success. An island nation separated from the Asian mainland by a hundred or more miles of rough sea, Japan has only succumbed to one invasion -- that of the United States in 1945. Thus, the Japanese have been able to develop their nation without much outside interference. If one compares the relatively peaceful history of Japan with that of such violence-prone regions as Israel/Palestine or northern China, Japan's advantage is readily apparent.

Japan's relative isolation has led to the development of an ethnically and linguistically uniform and united nation. There are none of the ethnic, religious, or linguistic disputes that have troubled India, Ireland, Quebec, or Belgium in recent decades. Except for relatively brief periods of civil strife, Japan has been ruled effectively by military and civilian governments in

Kyoto and, more recently, Tokyo. Thus, Japan has had a peaceful history under the unified rule of one government for much of its history.

Japan's Confucian tradition is also partially responsible for its strength. According to the Confucian world order espoused for centuries by the Chinese, there is a hierarchy among people and nations and both must know their proper place in the natural order of things. Peace, stability, and harmony are the goals of the Confucians. These goals can be attained if everybody understands his rank and role and behaves accordingly. A superior will have the honor, respect and devotion of a follower, but to earn the respect and obedience of an inferior, the leader must provide good ethical leadership. The superior becomes a loving and kind father who cherishes all of his "children" and who is totally devoted to their welfare. The ruler governs by setting solid moral examples which inferiors must follow. The prime requisites for leadership are honor, sincerity, and education. In China, leaders were not chosen because of their status at birth. Instead, there was a rigid examination system that any talented and aspiring male could enter.

On an international level, China assumed the role of father and teacher. It regarded itself as a superior civilization whose responsibility was to spread the benefits of its better way of life to less fortunate, smaller, and weaker peoples around its periphery. Other nations were welcome to learn from China's example, but they were also supposed to show some respect for the superior Chinese nation. This attitude was sufficient while China remained the greatest military and economic power in the region, but it became disastrous during the seventeenth century when China began to encounter technologically superior people from the West. Chinese leaders saw little need to emulate the British in the construction of a modern navy because of the inferior status of the British "barbarians." The Chinese attitude of cultural superiority led to a century of rejection of anything modern and allowed the West to destroy much of traditional China.

Japan occupied the other end of the Confucian equation. Although it never was under any direct form of Chinese control, Japan's leaders acknowledged China's cultural and technological superiority and on several occasions made a strong effort to learn as much as they could from the

Chinese. Japan saw itself as an inferior and weak nation whose survival depended upon how much it could learn from the outside world. Thus, when the West threatened Japan in the nineteenth century, most Japanese recognized the technological superiority of the West and a new government was formed in 1868 that modernized along Western lines. This feeling of inferiority made the Japanese learn about the outsideworld and work hard to catch up with the West.

Japanese Confucianism differs greatly from Chinese Confucian tradition in the respect that there is little emphasis on the need for ethical government. Rather,the stress is on the need for loyalty and devotion by the people in their attitudes toward the government.[7] There is, however, a strong Confucian tradition in the Japanese veneration of education and educational achievement despite the fact that leadership in Japan was primarily hereditary and the Chinese examination system was never seriously adopted by any Japanese government. Some estimates place the male literacy rate at forty or fifty percent in the middle of the nineteenth century, giving Japan a well-educated, united, and disciplined citizenry to face the threat from the Western powers. Thus, the Japanese have developed a tradition of quality education and educational attainment coupled with a sense of order, obedience, and discipline that they still exhibit today.

Japan experienced a lengthy social and economic revolution during the Meiji period (1868-1912). The new government that seized power from the tottering Tokugawa Shogunate in 1868 consisted of young, well-educated and intensely nationalistic *samurai*[8] who were determined to preserve Japan's independence. Their revolution was based on the notion that if Japan was to survive, it had to modernize every aspect of society. The heart of the nation had to be changed along with the outer trimmings. This attitude was substantially different from that of the Chinese government in the late nineteenth century, which believed that China could preserve its independence if it purchased a few battleships rather than make substantial changes to its overall way of life. Japan's successful revolution, which was carefully led from the top by government leaders, consisted primarily of efforts to modernize the nation's educational system, to develop modern industry, and to build a new army and navy.

The efforts at education were central to Japan's revolution. Many young Japanese were sent to study in the United States and in Europe, and the Japanese government hired numerous young American and European teachers to train Japanese. The emphasis in this educational effort, which began in the late 1860s and early 1870s, was on foreign languages, natural science, and math. Foreign teachers in Japan were put in charge of schools, where they trained carefully selected intelligent students in these fields. These students entered government service and industry or, more commonly, became school teachers to pass on the fruits of their education to the Japanese masses. By 1900 Japan had a universal educational system through the elementary years and a respectable number of high schools, colleges, and universities.

The revolution in industry was also led in part by the government. Japan began with light industry and competed successfully in world markets in the production of textiles and silk. The development of heavy industry, however, was also carefully planned. In many instances, the government built a model plant based on Western technology and then sold the plant at a very low price to a group of entrepreneurs who would then run the factory with government supervision or advice. By 1900 there were a good number of modern mines, shipyards, munitions plants, iron and steel mills, and railways across Japan, in addition to many textile mills. Japan had already become an industrial power.

The development of a strong and modern army and navy were also important in the Meiji government's plans. Universal military service was required of all men. There was considerable help from the Germans in the development of the army and from the British in the construction of a new navy. The armed forces were soon put into action in two wars -- against China in 1894-95 and against Russia a decade later -- as Japan began its efforts at carving out an empire on the Asian mainland.

At the start of the twentieth century Japanese leaders faced a real dilemma: should Japan seek an empire in Asia or should it refrain from imperialist activities? There were two factors in the eventual decision in favor of expansion. The first was the fear that unless Japan had its own sphere of influence, it would be strangled by such Western states as Germany and Russia, which were expanding rapidly in northern China. The Korean peninsula, which faced Japan's southwestern flank like a hostile "dagger," was especially worrisome to the Japanese government. Japan was so fearful of a foreign takeover of Korea that it fought two wars with China and Russia to gain control of Korea and surrounding areas in southern Manchuria. A secondary factor that contributed to Japan's imperialistic endeavors was the need to acquire natural resources and farm land for its surplus farming population.

The tragedy of twentieth century Japan is the fact that it became preoccupied with its Asian empire. It exploited Korea with little outside intervention or protest, but its efforts in China were less successful. Each time the Japanese acquired control over a new piece of territory deeper into China, it became necessary to expand Japan's arc of defense to defend the newly acquired territory. And, of course, most Chinese were not exactly thrilled with the idea of having parts of their country occupied by foreign powers. In the 1920s and early 1930s so many Chinese resisted Japanese expansion that tens of thousands of Japanese troops were sent to China. Japan's goal was not to conquer China as a whole, but to gain control over a compliant Chinese government. The struggle for China eventually expanded into full scale war between China and Japan and contributed greatly to the expanded Pacific War that began in 1941 with the bombing at Pearl Harbor.

Postwar Japan

World War II wiped out many of the gains that Japan had made since the Meiji Restoration of 1868. Four decades after the end of World War II, however, Japan is once again a world power. Why has Japan been so successful?

One factor that explains why Japan has prospered in recent years is that the Japanese were shocked into action. The bombed-out factories and cities of Japan meant the destruction of plants that needed to be replaced in the next two decades anyway. The new factories were equipped with the best and most modern machines which gave the Japanese an initial competitive advantage over the victor states, whose older factories were still being used. More important was that millions of former soldiers took off their uniforms and put on boiler suits with a new national purpose -- "more-more rather than war-war."[9] Men came home from the war with a new national purpose -- to rebuild Japan. Japan had a highly disciplined and educated work force that became the nucleus of its modernization and recovery efforts.

Japan's successful postwar educational system is the key reason for Japan's continued success. Very high literacy rates and excellent educational standards are the major reasons for Japan's success in meeting the challenge of a technologically advanced West a century ago and for Japan's economic leadership today. It is a very rigorous system that provides not only an excellent education for those students who make it to the better universities, but also a strong dose of discipline and dedication to all students. When a former student enters the work force, he is already well-trained and disciplined for a lifetime of dedicated hard work at a corporation.

Japan's success can also be attributed to the simple fact that the people work very hard. A Japanese government commission recently proposed reducing the workweek to 40 hours from the current 48 hours, but it is being opposed by workers. The habit of working long hours, often without overtime, is ingrained in the Japanese from their days as students. According to the Japanese Labor Ministry in 1985, Japanese workers averaged 2,110 hours on the job last year, compared with 1,850 in the United States and Britain and 1,650 in France. And though the average worker is entitled to 12 national holidays a year, he usually takes only seven off. Japan's massive trade surpluses are being blamed on too much work and too little pleasure. Too little work elsewhere might have something to do with those surpluses, too.

New equipment and a disciplined and educated workforce gave Japan an initial advantage, but these factors alone cannot explain Japan's enduring success. There are other factors which have also contributed greatly to Japan's growth. Japanese corporations have been very successful for other reasons and it is their success that has brought wealth, power, and success to Japan. The outstanding success of many Japanese corporations (*kaisha*) is a result of a highly competitive strategy that differs greatly from their American counterparts. Authors of such noted books as *Theory Z*[10] attribute Japan's success to special characteristics of management or culture which give the Japanese a special advantage over the United States. Japan's management system works very well within the nation's consensus-oriented society, but the system cannot by itself account for the financial success of so many *kaisha*. Ultimately it is the company that takes risks, competes for markets, and trades and competes with foreign competitors; ultimatelyit is the *kaisha* that makes the profit and pays the workers.

James C. Abegglen and George Stalk, Jr., authors of the recent book *Kaisha: The Japanese Corporation* [11], list the following four "competitive fundamentals" chosen by successful Japanese corporations. They are

1. A growth bias.
2. A preoccupation with actions of competitors.
3. The creation and ruthless exploitation of competitive advantage.
4. The choice of corporate financial and personnel policies that are economically consistent with all ofthe preceding.[12]

Abegglen and Stalk correctly insist that the strong bias towards growth of the *kaisha* comes from their births during periods of upward economic acceleration. Those companies that grew quickly and that took chances and successfully competed against less growth-oriented companies were the survivors. Those that failed to follow this pattern either went bankrupt or shifted to other areas of production. For example, during the 1950s there were as many as forty to fifty producers of motorcycles in Japan, but successful growth strategies by the Honda Motor Corporation forced the others to withdraw from the manufacture of motorcycles.

Product diversification is an essential ingredient of the growth patterns of many Japanese *kaisha*; however, in the United States a company faced with a decrease in demand for one of its product lines will resort instead to cutbacks in production and layoffs of many employees. This was certainly the case in the early 1970s when the importation of Japanese cars into the United States threatened American automobile companies. Parts of Detroit became deserted. In December, 1986, AT&T, facing the challenge from other competitors in the phone business, announced the impending layoff of 27,000 workers. Many AT&T workers had felt secure in their jobs. It has been said that AT&T represented stability and that if you worked for

"Ma Bell," you had a job for life. The fact that "Ma Bell" is in trouble is a danger sign for the whole American economy.

In Japan, wholesale layoffs of workers in response to weakened demand was unheard of until the mid-1980s. The traditional Japanese approach by a company facing weakened demand in one field would be to either increase demand in that field or to find another area in which the capacity of the organization could be better utilized. Abegglen and Stalk mention the famous case of Canon, the famous producer of Japanese cameras. Canonwas once exclusively a producer of cameras, but was threatened by a drop in demand for its main product. It responded by diversifying its line of production and started making printers, computers, word processors, facsimile machines, copiers, and semiconductor manufacturing equipment. Today cameras represent less than a third of Canon's sales.[13] This is a marked contrast to American and German camera companies that have generally scaled back or closed their operations.

Japanese companies with a growth bias will make decisions and implement plans that are designed explicitly to produce growth. They add physical and human capacity ahead of demand. Prices are not set at what the market will bear. Rather, prices are set at a point where the public will begin buying the product, thereby increasing the company's market share.[14]

Actively seeking market share rather than a quick movement toward profit is vital to a Japanese company. For example, when the first video cassette recorders (VCR) and compact audio discs (CD) were produced a few years ago, they were extremely expensive. Prices in the United States for these devices were well over $1000, effectively keeping them out of the hands of the average American family. American and European companies failed to lower prices; instead, they sat back to see how market demand would go. Japanese companies such as Sony and Matsushita, however, greatly increased demand by slashing prices and vastly increasing production which, in turn, lowered the overall cost of each set. The Japanese found themselves far ahead in a business that doubled in volume every year. The Japanese *kaisha* and a growing number of Korean firms now almost totally dominate the production of VCRs and CDs.

In summary, when demand in a market sector is weak, a *kaisha* with a growth bias will step up their levels of investment. Product variety is increased, prices are cut, and distribution is expanded.

A second preoccupation of the *kaisha* is the condition of its competitors. People sometimes talk of the world of Japan, Inc. where all Japanese work harmoniously toward a common goal. Nothing could be further from the truth. The world of Japanese business is extremely competitive and only the fittest survive. Survival depends upon staying ahead of or equal to thec ompetition, but never, never falling behind. The objectives of Japanese companies are summarzied in the following slogan:

"Be better, not behind;

If not better, be different."[15]

Thus, if a Japanese company in one sector of the economy comes up with a new product of consequence, its competitors will try to produce a better or cheaper version of the same product. If they are unable to do that, they will produce, if possible, an interesting variation of the old product. For example, a few years ago Sony created a sensation by producing a miniature television set. It sold well at a fairly high price, but then other Japanese companies began producing cheaper versions of the same product. Sony then movedon to other areas and made a fortune with its innovative and highly profitable Walkman.

A third area of Japanese success is ruthless exploitation of competitive advantage. The point is not to be good at everything; rather, the Japanese put a lot of energy into dominating selected fields where they can do very well. Today the Japanese have focused their attention on creating competitive advantage through product line variety, high quality, and technological innovation. The Japanese have produced a narrow line of products in very focused factories. Thus, if it is properly focused, a small factory with a narrow productline can have substantially lower costs than a much bigger factory producing a much wider line of products.[16] A vast amount of research and development of new products has led to command of whole new areas of manufacturing such as electronics.

The fourth area where the Japanese *kaisha* do well is the use of corporate financial and personal policies that are economically consistent with a bias towards growth. Availability of cash is crucial. Where the *kaisha* differ from their Western competitors is in the amount of money that they borrow and in their attitudes towards dividends and profits. This results from the fact that the Japanese save much more than their Western counterparts and banks have a great deal of money to lend out at low rates.

In Japan, household financial savings have been deposited in banks, postal savings, and life insurance policies. Financial institutions that serve as depositories of personal savings make loans to borrowers, principally business firms. The Japanese government adopted a low interest policy immediately after World War II and placed ceilings on loan rates.[17] Thus, funds were, and still are, readily available to Japanese firms. Japanese firms had a gross operating surplus of 35 percent from 1975-83.[18]

A major reason for the Japanese urge to save relatively large percentages of their earnings is that the Japanese government provides few social services for the citizenry. There is an excellent national health system, but little else. As late as 1970, for example, only 5.7 percent of Japanese gross national product was devoted to social welfare as compared to 10.7 percent in the United States and 20.6 percent in Sweden. The attitude of the Japanese government has been that living standards of all in society can be raised by encouraging rapid economic growth. In recent years the Japanese government has passed some legislation to move the nation toward the achievement of a welfare system comparable in many respects to those of other advanced nations, but it still lags far behind in some areas, such as social security.

As a result of relatively low tax rates and a paucity of social services, Japanese workers have felt constrained to save as much as 20 percent of their incomes.[19] In 1983, the average worker saved 20.9 percent of his disposable income while farmers saved 19.4 percent. This figure was lower than in 1975, when workers saved 23 percent of their income and farmers saved 25.8 percent.[20] This drop in savings is probably a result of increases in income taxes and social security payments imposed in 1975.[21] However, Japanese banks still have a great deal more disposable cash than many Western banks. To make money, these Japanese banks are willing to lend out money at a much lower rate than is found in the United States.[22]

Big business in Japan receives much of its financing from bank loans. The higher returns of equity of the Japanese manufacturer are not achieved without some risk. The leverage, or amount of borrowed funds compared to the amount of equity funds, of the average Japanese manufacturing firm has been about 2:1 for the 1970s, compared with a debt-to-equity ratio of 0.5:1 for the average American firm.[23] Japanese firms do notraise much capital through the sale of stocks. Borrowing from banks means that Japanese firms are not dependent upon the whims of Wall Street investors. Some of the most successful products made by Japanese companies were not profitable when they first came out. For example, the Kentucky Fried Chicken franchise in Japan lost money for at least the first eighteen quarters that it operated in Japan. But since the Japanese companies borrowed money from banks rather than selling shares to stockholders, immediate profits were not a great concern. Japanese bankers were happy as long as the firm made payments each month and the company increased the market share of its various new products.

Thus, the Japanese have the luxury of time to nurse their products along, improving on their quality and making other changes to meet public demand. The financiers of Kentucky Fried Chicken in Japan were content to continue lending money as long as KFC continued to expand its stores, increase public awareness, and make changes in the food it served to meet Japanese tastes. The manufacture of automobiles was also made more profitable by long-term investments. In the 1950s and 1960s Japanese car producers invested tremendous sums of money in building small fuel-efficient cars at a time when there was no real market for them in the United States. By the fuel crisis of the mid-1970s, however, the Japanese had enough time to perfect their cars and there was a ready market in the West. Losses were turned into very healthy profits.

Many American companies do not have the advantage of long-term planning. When they issue stocks on Wall Street, their products have to show fairly quick and healthy profits or else their stocks will be sold. Few shareholders in the United States would willingly tolerate eighteen down quarters from a concern like KFC. This fact gives Japanese concerns a tremendous advantage over American competitors.

The Japanese corporations have also flourished due to their employment and personnel policies. The *kaisha* employs a fairly small number of permanent employees who are chosen for their educational backgrounds, overall skills, and personal attributes. These permanent employees will remain with the company until their retirement forty years later. Consequently, the *kaisha* can invest a great amount of money in their training knowing that, unlike many American workers who may take their newly acquired skills to different and often better jobs, its investment in the workers will not be lost. Japanese employees thus spend a great deal of time in training programs and become proficient in a wide range of areas. Rather than being a specialist just in accounting, for example, a Japanese employee will know a great deal about many facets of his company and can perform many tasks. Thus, if there is a temporary need for another accountant, the business office can borrow an employee from another branch of the corporation. There is no need to hire a new accountant from the outside.

Japanese firms hire a great many women, but until very recently, it was rare for women to become permanent employees. Most young women out of high school or college only work for a few years before retiring because of marriage and childbirth. They may return to part-time or temporary jobs after their children enter school. Women, however, are paid much less than men and do not get the same benefits. In other words, Japanese corporations have little commitment towards their female employees and pay them very little. Women are a source of very cheap labor for Japanese companies.

Another exploited worker is the temporary employee "borrowed" from one of the company's many small support firms. There is still a "dual economy" in Japan with the large and very successful *kaisha* at the top surrounded by dozens of small companies that provide a vast array of support services for the *kaisha*. For example, a large automobile company may assemble cars in its plants and sell them under its logo, but many parts, including windows and carpets, are made by the smaller support companies. In times of rapid expansion, the corporation does not have to hire masses of new, very costly, permanent employees. Rather, it borrows temporary workers from some of the support companies. When production slackens, the *kaisha* will return the workers to their original firms. Using workers where they are needed means there is less unemployment and thus there is less need to pay unemployment benefits, although a decline in such areas as steel led to growing unemployment in 1987.

Another factor that gives the Japanese company a distinct advantage over many American firms is the idea of "just on time delivery." This system, which began with Toyota in the 1950s, was aimed at reducing the time of changing from the production of one part or model to another. The thought was that if changeover time could be lowered substantially, changeovers would be made much more frequently. More models could be made, run lengths could be shortened, inventories could be minimized, and workers would be idle for less time. Thus the negative effects of greatly increasing variety could be reduced.[24]

An important goal of Japanese manufacturers is to lower the time and expense of keeping large inventories. One danger of inventory build-up is that the time required to reduce it continues to grow, and with this increase in holding time comes an increase in the average handling and storage cost per unit. For example, if Toyota needs a certain number of engine parts per day, that many parts are delivered on a daily basis at a fixed time. However, when the diminishing setup and run cost per unit are added to the growing handling and storage cost per unit, a run length can be determined for which the sum of those costs is minimized.[25] Avoiding inventory build-up is yet another means used by the Japanese to lower production costs and gain a competitive edge over American counterparts.

Other Success Factors:

Japan's stable pro-business political climate is also an important key to Japan's postwar economic success. Conservative parties have controlled Japan's Diet (national legislature) since 1948. The ruling Liberal-Democratic Party (LDP) sponsors a pro-business program and has kept corporate taxes and social spending low. That has encouraged personal saving and corporate growth. Japan is a strong democratic state with adominant ruling party and a number of vocal opposition parties which at various times have controlled a few local or prefectural governments, but voters seem content to let the conservatives stay in power because of their success in managing Japan's economy.

Low defense spending and continued American military assistance have also helped Japan. The American-written constitution of Japan that came into force in 1947 includes a provision that Japan shall not have any armed forces. There is, in fact, a small Japanese Self-Defense force with just under 300,000 members, but, in reality, Japan depends upon the United States for its defense. Today, the United States pays dearly for the defense of Japan, and one must not also forget all of the direct assistance the United States gave the Japanese in the late 1940s and 1950s.

Weaknesses in the Japanese System:

While there are many obvious success factors in the Japanese system, in the mid-1980s several economists and commentators on the Japanese economy stressed that the Japanese economy is beginning to show signs of weakness and decline. According to Hiroshi Kato, a former official in Japan's Ministry of International Trade and Industry (MITI), "No country can enjoy prosperity forever. The whole system is breaking down. We can't go out and get the growth we used to. The feeling is that Japan is in the beginnings of decline."[26]

Jon Woronoff in his book, *Inside Japan, Inc.*, notes that starting in the early 1980s, the once lofty growth rate of the Japanese economy has shrunk well below five percent. Japan, he notes, has become a high cost economy and productivity has not been rising fast enough to compensate for rising costs. New trends include high personal debt and a drop in personal income. Japan's economy has matured; people have all of the basic requirements of life and do not feel obliged to purchase large numbers of cars or television sets. Accompanying the drop in domestic sales is a labor force which is becoming increasingly older.[27] By the start of the next century Japan will have the oldest population among the modern industrialized nations with a chronic shortage of young workers and a large number of older people in need of expensive care.

Another perhaps more serious problem seems to be the attitude of younger workers. As noted earlier, Japanese continue to work very hard, certainly much harder than their peers in the West, but for some workers there seems to be less enthusiasm. At least some Japanese workers seem to have lost the "Yamato Damashi" or "Japanese Spirit" which is the notion that, with the correct spirit, Japan can prevail against all odds.[28] Until the 1980s, the Japanese worker was one who worked six days a week and ten hours a day for the good of his company and nation. Turning Japan into the world's leading economic power was a goal that they were supposedly aspiring for. Whether or not there is any validity to this idea is hard to say, but in the first three or four decades after World War II, Japanese worked very hard, but now one sees a growing breakdown of this work ethic. More young and middle-aged workers seem to want to spend more time at home with their families and in the pursuit of leisure. They are far wealthier than in the past and they want to enjoy the fruits of their labor. [29]

Japan may be following the footsteps of the United States, Great Britain and other Western nations which have been affected by younger people who have rebelled against the work habits and expectations of their elders. These nations have paid a stiff price for this rebellion in terms of less attention to education and greater alienation at the work place. Japan is behind the West in this development, but in the Japanese press one does hear more accounts of violence in the classroom, rebellion against the current entrance examination system, and anger at the current work system which squelches individuality. A younger Japanese worker will find that there is little room for individual creativity in the workplace. Still locked into the mentality of mass production, export-led creativity, and traditional hierarchies, the *kaisha* to some extent also adhere to the traditional system of promotion that moves all people of a similar entering year (class) up at the same time regardless of skill. A younger worker with ambition may have to wait thirty years before reaching a position with real seniority. In a nation where individualism is becoming more pronounced, this can be a depressing prospect. As one manager at Hitachi recently noted, "It's frightening to watch young people work these days. There is no initiative, no ambition, no hope. People are at work, but seeming only to show up. I fear we can no longer depend on the Japanese spirit, and without the Japanese spirit, where will we be?[30]

Kenichi Ohmae, managing director of the Tokyo office of the management consultant firm of McKinsey & Co., is one of a growing number of skeptics who challenge the notion that Japan's success can endure much longer. In a recent article in the *Baltimore Sun*, he noted:

> Many economists say that the United States today is in a situation alarmingly similar to 1929. But Japan, far more than America, is close to plunging into a depression that, with double-digit unemployment, could severely strain a society that counts lifetime employment as a virtual right of citizenship.
>
> Real estate prices provide one of the more obvious signs of Japan's troubles and rising social pressures. A few years ago, many of America's babyboomers despaired of ever owning their own homes because prices seemed to be rising so fast. But most of them managed to buy their starter homes, begin families, and move ahead. Not in Japan.
>
> By the time a young couple here is ready to settle down, a home is probably beyond their reach. Real estate prices in Tokyo have risen an average of 300 percent in the last two and a half years. As a result we are creating a new proletariat -- people with little hope that they will possess any property in their lifetime.
>
> We are also creating many millionaires. Until recently, Japan was 90% middle class. It was a happy, growth-oriented nation. Today, there is a growing polarization between those who have invested in their education and now rent small apartments and those who own and speculate with property.
>
> While, thanks to the yen-dollar exchange rate, Japan has the highest per capita gross national product in the world, ($18,000) living standards for most Japanese have improved little. To enjoy the same standard of living as an American couple, a Japanese couple would have to spend an average of 35 percent more -- twice as much to maintain cars and 50 percent more on utilities and food.
>
> And the brilliance of Japan's economic progress could fade as quickly as it appeared. Americans tend to think that all Japanese industries are competitive, but this is far from true. We are about to face, by any standard set in developed countries, widespread unemployment. Add up all the employees in Japanese industries that are strong world-wide -- automobiles, machinery, electronics, and steel -- and they amount to only 7 percent of the work force. The others work in less competitive and sometimes protected industries.
>
> Today's unemployment rate in manufacturing of about 3 percent will climb by two percentage points as a result of increased imports, assuming the current exchange rate

continues. Reduced exports will likely add to the unemployment rate, raising the overall rate in the manufacturing sector to 7.5 percent. If Japan were to reduce rice and other agricultural trade barriers, unemployment could reach 13 percent.

Ironically, one of our biggest problems is that we have too much money. Our individual savers generate more than $1 billion a day while our companies pile up about $500 million a day. This money once financed plants and facilities, but no longer. Japan's industrial overcapacity has created tensions internationally, and Japanese companies are not building plants at home.

That is Japan's Catch-22. Plenty of money and nowhere to invest it except in more money. Companies have so much money that they are building foreign exchange trading floors instead of adding production lines, reasoning that it is better to make money with money than to make profitless products that cause retaliation and resentment abroad.

The situation is not hopeless, however. We have our fundamental lessons to learn from America. First, we must deregulate. Thousands of intrusive regulations strangle our customers. The Ministry of Transportation, perhaps the champion regulator, has more than 2,000 regulations, including such rules as a mandatory $650 auto inspection every two years. In the United States, if you want to move yourself, you simply rent a U-Haul truck or trailer. Not in Japan. Here you have to get a license to use a trailer. Of course, you have to have a driver's license, too. Those cost a tidy $2,000.

Along with the high cost of housing, regulations are the primary reason we are rich only on paper. One of our first steps toward improving our standard of living is to remove them.

But it takes many years to take power away from government.

Like the United States, Japan is making the fundamental mistake of liberalizing its markets in a piece-meal fashion. Creeping up on closed markets and opening them a few at a time kills the wrong industries for the wrong reasons. For example, if the Japanese biscuit market were opened, our local companies would be destroyed by imports from Denmark and elsewhere. Our biscuit makers would be handicapped by the high cost of regulated domestic wheat. On the other hand, if we liberalized wheat markets we could keep the biscuit makers working. They are, in fact, efficient and competitive manufacturers.

By opening manufacturers to competition while protecting raw-materials producers, we destroy the wrong people. Japan has done this too often in response to the complaints of foreign exporters.

Unfortunately, all this takes time, and time is growing exceedingly short. In fact, Japan may be facing a vicious cycle. Our continuing trade imbalances will result in a stronger yen, which will lead to higher unemployment. The corresponding shortfall of tax revenue will restrict government spending, causing a contraction of domestic demand. That will force our companies once again to resort to export markets. Their efforts to exploit foreign markets will result either in the closing of those markets or larger trade imbalances and an even stronger yen.

Within this spiral, speculation in foreign exchange will live a life of its own, divorced from the economy, until it leads to an economic breakdown.

While there is much truth to Mr. Ohmae's comments, he almost completely ignores the political realities of modern Japan. For example, the ruling Liberal-Democratic Party (LDP) has a vested interest in supporting farmers who in turn vote heavily for LDP candidates in a gerry mandered parliamentary system that gives more weight to rural than urban districts. On the other hand, Japan is receiving intense pressure from the United States and other Western states to liberalize trade. Thus, the Japanese government must learn to workin a political environment where seemingly irrational decisions have to be made and where some groups such as the nation's biscuit makers might have to be sacrificed. In this instance Mr. Ohmae also fails to mention the obvious fact that if the wheat market in Japan were liberalized to suit the needs of biscuit makers, Japan's wheat farmers would be seriously hurt. Deregulation, if it comes, must come slowly.

Mr. Ohmae is correct when he asserts that the price of real estate in Tokyo and other urban areas where most of the Japanese population lives has created difficulties for younger members of a culture where home ownership has been a cherished dream for generations. Japan's increasing number of corporations with vast amounts of excess cash on hand are largely to blame. Inthe mid-1980s Tokyo became the world's new financial center. Japanese banks and corporations bought or constructed office buildings or office suites for investment purposes and many foreign companies began flocking to Tokyo. All available office space was quickly occupied and the value of central Tokyo real estate started its climb. People living in the center of the city sold out and, with the hope of avoiding large capital gains taxes, plowed their profits into nearby high-class residential areas which raised real estate prices there. This wave of speculation and astounding price hikes for land has spread far out into the Tokyo suburbs and neighboring cities.[31]

The astronomical hike in land values means that the total value of land in Japan, a nation only five percent the size of the United States, is now twice that of the entire land mass of the United States. Unfortunately, while Japan is widely reported to have become the richest country in the world, most people cannot afford to buy their own homes anymore. The result is that residents of Tokyo and other Japanese cities are being divided into groupings of haves and have-nots, thus threatening to put to an end to the much vaunted sharing of success that has characterized Japanese society in the postwar era.[32]

For the present, younger Japanese couples seeking a home anywhere near Tokyo may as well give up. According to the Japan Real Estate Institute, the average salaried worker in the market for a house in the late 1980s is 38 years old, earns about $40,000 a year, and has saved about $50,000. Banks or lending companies would recommend the purchase of a house valued at $175,000, but there is no house or apartment of any size to be had for such a price.[33] People who meet these characteristics generally live in small three or four room (one bedroom) apartments in outlying areas of Tokyo that rent for about $700-$900 a month.

If this page were a prime piece of Tokyo property, it would cost about 1.8 million yen (about $14,400) in 1987. On the other hand, if this page had been part of a recent land deal in the center of London, it would have gone for $3,400.[34] Property, perhaps more than anything else except a drink in a bar in the Ginza, is extremely expensive in Japan.

Mr. Ohmae is not entirely correct in asserting that living standards of the Japanese have not improved. Yes, housing is a very real problem which will only be alleviated when more farmland is converted to industrial and housing uses. On the other hand, the Japanese are buying more cars than ever before, are vacationing more for longer periods of time, are dining out more, and are purchasing more of the luxuries of life. The number of Japanese traveling abroad has risen dramatically in recent years to an estimated 6.5 million in 1987 -- a sure sign of rising prosperity.[35] People who cannot afford real estate are spending their money in other ways. Certain segments of the economy are suffering, but overall the long-term prognosis for Japan looks quite good. Ohmae offers no evidence to support his thesis that Japan will soon plunge into a deep depression, but his comments on the polarization of society over the question of housing are right on target.

The situation for Japan, however, is still far from hopeless. Economic growth does continue, unemployment is still down, and most industries in high tech and other more modern fields continue to post handsome profits. There are also very handsome profits to be made from Japan's investments abroad -- projected to be $400 billion by 1990. Japan, however, should not become increasingly dependent on financial services for its continued prosperity. Great Britain lived off its vast overseas holdings for most of the first half of this century, but when these collapsed, there was nothing left. Britain is economically a dying or already dead nation. Japan must be careful to avoid the mistakes that have doomed former economic giants like Great Britain.[36]

TWO SUCCESSFUL FIRMS: HONDA AND SONY

An analysis of Japan's success should also include a brief discussion of the development of one or two Japanese firms. Capsule histories of two Japanese companies familiar to many foreigners, Sony and Honda, are described below. While they may not be typical of many Japanese companies in all respects, one can trace in their development much of the ingenuity, dedication, and hard work that has made Japan a great economic power today.

HONDA:

Japanese society resembles a great wheel. In the center near the hub one will find those traditional societal elements which fail to move much as the wheel moves forward in time. On the other edge you will find Japan's mavericks, its innovators. They are spun off the edges by traditional Japan's conservatism, it spronounced xenophobia, and its instincts for individual conformity and group consensus. But it is these dissidents spun off to the outer edges of the Japanese establishment who give the wheel its hard cutting edge. Innovative Japanese companies like Honda, Yashica, and Sony are at the outer rim of the business world and give Japan much of its economic muscle.

One of Japan's great industrial innovators is Soichiro Honda, founder of the Honda Motor Corporation.[37] He was born in 1906 in Hammamatsu in Shizuoka Prefecture, the son of a blacksmith. Honda was a notoriously bad student in school, as his interests were centered elsewhere. He wrote that "Even before I started school, I was fond of fumbling with machinery and was interested in engines."[38] In his youth he resembled Tom Sawyer, since his childish pranks often got him into trouble; however, his interest in mechanics continued and in 1922 he left home to work in an automobile repair shop in Tokyo. By 1925 he was a master mechanic with his own shop in Hamamatsu.

His business grew, as did his reputation as one of Japan's leading authorities on automobile mechanics. He attempted a number of improvements for automobile parts and soon succeeded in making strong cast-metal spokes for wheels to replace the wooden spokes then in use in Japan. In the late 1930s he went into manufacturing and developed a machine that could mechanically produce airplane propellers. This cut the time it took to produce a propeller from one week to 30 minutes. His invention and production were critical to Japan's ability to wage war both in China and in the Pacific. Japan's ability to strike so effectively at Pearl Harbor was in part due to Honda's contributions to the Japanese cause.

Honda prospered during the early part of the Pacific War, but his factories and resources were destroyed in the last stages of the war. Although his financial empire was in ruins, Honda refused to give up amidst the physical destruction and emotional gloom that dominated Japan in the months and years following the end of World War II.

After World War II, Honda realized that the Japanese would need a cheap and reliable form of transportation. By attaching surplus gasoline motors to bicycles, he founded the Honda Motor Corporation. He worked closely with partner Fujisawa Takeo to make better machines based on the following three requirements:

[1] The new motor had to be practical, something everybody in need of a cheap form of transportation could use;

[2] it had to be maneuverable;

[3] it had to have a small but powerful engine.

The result of their work was the C-100, called the Super-Cub in Japan, but known throughout the world as the "step-through" motorbike. It was to become one of the most famous transportation devices in the world, rivaling, in its own way, Henry Ford's Model T automobile. Much of its success was due to the fact that it was a machine almost everyone could both drive and afford. Honda's vehicle not only revolutionized his own company, but by 1960 it dominated the world's business in that field.

Honda and his company still dominate the motorcycle industry, but the leaders of Honda have turned their attention elsewhere as well. Honda's overall success in selling automobiles at home has not been that great, but Honda has been very successful in North America and other automobile export markets in the mid-1980s. Many Honda cars are now being produced at the Honda plant in Maryville, Ohio. The Honda Motor Company's "stratified charge engine," which it calls the CVCC, is noted for its low pollution and high gasoline economy. In the 1970s the engine became one of the new innovations in automobile technology amidst global concerns over increased pollution and shortages in petroleum. The fact that this once small company was able to offer imaginative devices to help weather the fuel crisis contrasts with the lack of foresight exhibited by Detroit and Europe and is indicative of the innovativeness of Japanese industry today.

SONY:

> "Sony's Challenge! Profits are falling, competition is intense, and the strong yen makes everything worse. At 66, Chairman Akio Morita is now working hard to reinvent the company he helped to start."[39]

The cover of the June 1, 1987 issue of *Business Week* displays the picture of Akio Morita, Chairman and founder of Sony, and the caption quoted above. The weak dollar and strong yen, intense competition from foreign rivals, and the failure of its Betamax have led to a genuine challenge to Sony's ability to survive in the long run.

Competition in consumer electronics is brutal: after having developed such hits as Trinitron televisions and Walkman tape players, Sony is now watchingthe hottest market pass it by. While Sony clung to its Betamax video recorder format, the rest of the world switched to VHS. The result has been a drastic decline in profits. Sony's overall worldwide sales declined 7% to $8.2 billion, while earnings from operations fell a stunning 75%. Earnings declined another 56% for the first 5 months of fiscal 1987 from a year earlier. Rival Matsushita Electrical Industrial Co., in contrast, endured a more manageable 44% drop in operating earnings in 1986. Measured in dollars, Sony's 1986 sales increased by 24%, but measured in yen, they declined by 11%. "The falling dollar has produced a nearly 50% tax on us," Morita complained to *Business Week.*

These recent reverses are the first in Sony's impressive postwar history. Until very recently perhaps no other electronics firm in the world has had as high a reputation as this relatively small Japanese firm whose innovative, quality products have so revolutionized the industry. A leader in its field for over four decades, Sony has created and then improved on new products and has won a market for its goods through shrewd programs to educate the public about their use. Its radios, television sets, and tape recorders have never been inexpensive, but their high quality and dependability have ensured the company's success.

Sony's fame and reputation, however, are newly won. In the late 1940s it was just one of the many tiny electronics firms which opened in Tokyo after the Pacific War ended in 1945. Founded by two young electronics engineers, Masaru Ibuka and Akio Morita, Sony's first home was in several rooms of a burned out department store in downtown Tokyo. Both men were skillful and intelligent workers who quickly established a good name for their company by producing and revising consoles for the Japanese government's NHK radiostations.[40]

The work for the NHK brought in an increasing number of customers, but Ibuka and Morita were dreamers with visions of creating new products that would bring them both fame and fortune. They had very little capital to invest in research and no real facilities to work in -- their first "factory" in Tokyo consisted of a few shacks that were so dilapidated that during a rainstorm executives had to work with umbrellas over their desks. A lengthy search for a new product that they could develop led to the production of Japan's first tape recorders.

One real problem for Sony's tiny staff was to find ways of instructing the Japanese public about the potential uses of the tape recorder. This education process necessitated hundreds of trips by Sony executives to schools, laboratories, government offices, and even street corner noodle shops whose owners were encouraged to get their customers to talk into them as an added form of entertainment. Schools and other purchasers began to buy these tape recorders by the thousands and Sony's reputation as an innovator was at last established.

It was not long before other Japanese firms began to produce tape recorders at more affordable prices; however, the high quality of Sony's equipment and the firm's dependability guaranteed it a continued good market. Nevertheless, Sony was not content to rest on its laurels. Its engineers later developed the world's first transistorized radios and television sets. Although Sony was a latecomer to Japan's television market, its novel Trinitron color sets marked a major advance in that field's technology.

Sony's innovativeness has not been confined solely to production. Its skillful research and ability to develop and keep large markets abroad have guaranteed it success. In fact, much of Sony's profit has come from foreign sales. Its executives have traveled extensively throughout the United States and Europe since the early 1950s exploring markets, determining what kinds of products would sell where, and promoting its goods with great skill. Overall, Sony has brilliantly marketed its products, although it did suffer a setback over production of the Betamax.

Sony's disastrous venture with the Betamax has caused the company to ponder how it might better its future prospects. As conceived, Betamax was a classic example of Sony's founding philosophy of looking for new markets where bigger, more established companies were not a threat. Sony correctly forecasted the immense latent demand for a machine that could both make and play back home videotapes, but it refused to yield when the

VHS format provided longer recording times and gradually became the industry standard. Sony officials claim that its Beta recorders provide a superior picture, but only one customer in twenty seeking a home video system buys Beta.[41]

The Beta debacle has forced Sony to alter its go-it-alone tradition whereby it stuck to the expensive, high-profit end of the market. Sony is now willing to use more conventional methods of sales/production of a certain good by going after market share. Thus, when recently it came time to price its portable compact disc player, Morita decreed that it must be less than 50,000 yen ($200). Even though the player cost more than that to produce, Morita correctly argued that the low price would generate enough sales to provide the volume production that would trigger economies of scale and profits. Sony is now pursuing market share strategy more diligently.

Sony is also cooperating more with competitors. For example, in developing the technology for compact disks and players, it has forged an alliance with Philips. It produces the 8mm equipment for the videoplayers marketed by Pioneer, Fuji, and others. In addition, Sony is making a major effort to diversify into nonconsumer businesses. Using its unique talents in video and semiconductor technology, Sony is creating its versions of future offices.[40]

Sony has suffered a bad shock, but it will undoubtedly recover since it is a small, flexible company with ready access to capital. Sony has no strong ties with the government of Japan's banks; it finances much of its own research and has a solid and independent financial bank. Sony's financial security coupled with its innovativeness will probably allow the company to survive into the next century.

CHAPTER I - NOTES

1.   *The Economist* (25 October 1986), p. 13.

2.   *The Japan Times Weekly* (19 April 1986), p. 10. Note: dollar values are approximate and are calculated on the yen valuation of $1.00 = 125 yen. The same exchange rate is used throughout this work. Readers should always refer to the yen value when evaluating figures presented here.

3.   Accurate comparisons are impossible because of the wildly fluctuating value of the dollar compared to the yen. Economists Martin Bronfenbrenner and Yasukichi Yasuba caution against the use of yen-dollar market exchange rates to calculate the real wealth and income of Japanese or other Americans. For example, such a method does not reflect purchasing power vis-a-vis non-traded goods, particularly services, which influence exchange rates extremely indirectly or not at all. For a discussion of international comparisons of real GNP (Gross National Product) and Per Capita Gross Domestic Product, see Bronfenbrenner and Yasuba, "Economic Warfare," in Kozo Yamamura and Yasukichi Yasuba, *The Political Economy of Japan: The Domestic Transformation* (Stanford:Stanford University Press, 1987), pp. 93-98.

4.   Source: NBC News "White Paper on Japan" broadcast (4 May 1987).

5.   *Asahi Nenkan 1986* (Tokyo: Asahi Shupansha, 1986), pp. 211-218.

6.   *Ibid.*, and *Japan Times Weekly* (11 July 1987), p.3.

7.   For an in depth discussion of this topic, see: Michio Morishima, *Why Japan 'Succeeded'?: Western Technology and the Japanese Ethos* (Cambridge: Cambridge University Press, 1982).

8.   Samurai were retainers of the *daimyo* (lords) until the formal end of feudalism early in the Meiji era. The samurai class performed most of the bureaucratic and clerical functions in many of the daimyo domains and were thus experienced and well educated as a class.

9.   *The Economist*, p. 13.

10.   William Ouchi, *Theory Z* (Reading, Mass.: Avon, 1982).

11.   James C. Abegglen and George Stalk, Jr., *Kaisha: The Japanese Corporation* (New York: Basic Books, 1985).

12.   *Ibid.*, p. 5.

13.   *Ibid.*, p. 6.

14.   *Ibid.*, pp. 6-7.

15.   *Ibid.*, p. 8.

16.   *Ibid.*, pp. 11-12.

17.   Kazuo Sato, "Saving and Investment" in Yamamura and Yasuba, p. 169.

18.   *Ibid.*, p. 170.

19.   The amount of savings for the family of a salaried worker in Tokyo was nearly triple of that of its debts. As of 1984 the average Japanese family with a salaried worker had 6.92 million yen (about $55,360) in savings accounts and 2.5 million yen (about $20,000) in debts. A survey by Dai-Ichi Kangyo in 1986 indicated an average household debt of 3.97 million yen ($31, 760) including money due for housing loans. Source: *The Japan Times Weekly* (April 19, 1986), p. 10.

20.   Sato, p. 148.

21.   *Ibid.*, p. 151.

22.   For example, in 1986 a friend in Tokyo received a large mortgage in Tokyo from a commercial bank at 7.7%, which is lower than the 10.5% rate I got the same year for my home in rural Virginia.

23.   Abegglen and Stalk, pp. 149-50.

24.   *Ibid.*, p. 94.

25.   *Ibid.*, p. 95.

26.   "Setting Sun?" in *The Washington Post*, 22 June 1986, p. 5.

27.   Jon Woronoff, *Inside Japan, Inc.* (Tokyo, 1983), pp. 212-231.

28.   "Setting Sun?" p. C4. This is typified by a letter I recently received from a friend in his late thirties who works on the senior staff of a large communications agency in Tokyo: "Frankly speaking, however, I prefer my family to this new job. In a sense, I will become what we call 'my home papa.'"

30.   "Setting Sun?", p. C4.

31.   *The Washington Post* (20 September 1987), p. A33.

32.   *Ibid.*

33.   *Ibid.*

34.   "Japanese Property, A Glittering Sprawl" in *The Economist* (3 October 1987), p. 25.

34.   "Japanese Property, A Glittering Sprawl" in *The Economist* (3 October 1987), p. 25.

35.   *Japan Times Weekly* (19 September 1987) p. 3.

36.   *Ibid*.

37.   For a useful study of Soichiro Honda's career, see Sol Sanders, *Honda: The Man and His Machines* (Tokyo: C.E. Tuttle, 1977).

38.   *Ibid*.

39.   "Sony's Challenge" in *Business Week* (1 June 1987), pp. 64-69.

40.   For an interesting history of Sony, see Akio Morita, *Made in Japan* (New York: Signet,1986), pp. 39-82.

41.   "Sony's Challenge", p. 67.

42.   *Ibid*.

CHAPTER II

COMMUNICATING WITH THE JAPANESE

Effective communication is the basis of a good business relationship. It pays to understand what your business partner is saying, but real communication is far more complicated than open verbal interchange. One must understand how the other person thinks and how he or she might react under a given set of circumstances. One must certainly be aware of the cultural differences between any two societies. Only when these factors are understood can a good business relationship start.

American relationships with Japan often have been hampered by a distinct communications gap between the two cultures. While there are occasional problems communicating within one's own cultural framework, there can be far greater problems when encountering people from other cultures. This in turn can lead to strains even in the best of relationships. Understanding a foreign culture begins with a knowledge of that culture's language, but while many Japanese learn English, few Westerners learn any Japanese.

Language:

Language is a distinct barrier between the United States and Japan. Americans have the impression that Japanese is a difficult language and only a few industrious souls have even attempted to master it. In some respects Japanese is an extremely difficult language, but in some ways it is easier than French or Spanish. It all depends on how one approaches the language and what one hopes to do with it. If a person wants to become fully proficient in Japanese so that he can read the *Asahi Shimbun* with ease, then many years of intensive study as well as a great deal of time spent in a fully Japanese environment are necessary. A diligent student who puts in many hours of study each week could make some sense out of France's *Le Monde* in six months or a year, but it would require many more years of work before he could fully digest the *Asahi Shimbun*. Part of the problem is that while

Americans only have to learn twenty-six letters in their alphabet, a reader of Japanese must know roughly two thousand *kanji* (Chinese characters) to be able to read a daily newspaper. On the other hand, if one seeks to learn enough conversational Japanese to be able to live in a Japanese neighborhood in Tokyo, to carry on basic conversations with Japanese, and to make oneself understood in many situations, then Japanese is indeed one of the simpler languages to learn. The pronunciation is extremely simple and the basic grammar is not complex. For example, the conjugation of verbs in Japanese is far simpler than in French or Spanish.[1]

Making an attempt to even master a few terms in Japanese is important for any business relationship. The Japanese prefer to do business with people whom they like and trust -- who show them some sympathy or consideration. The Japanese feel that their language is very difficult and are generally impressed when a foreigner makes some attempt to master even a small part of the language. Thus, even a few months of Japanese study can be most beneficial to an American doing business in Japan. At least he can get directions to the restroom and, more importantly, can impress the Japanese that he cares about them and their society. That is certainly the best way to make friends and influence people in Tokyo and Osaka.

Fortunately, however, it is not usually essential for the foreign businessman to be fully proficient in Japanese to do business in Japan. In most cases Japanese expect and actually strongly prefer to do business in English and will become upset when Americans try to do things entirely in Japanese. Unfortunately, although all educated Japanese learn some English as a written language, only a few Japanese have a good speaking knowledge of English unless they have spent some time abroad. A few companies send their more promising employees abroad for one or two years early in their careers, but unless you are meeting one of these individuals, chances for a highly sophisticated dialogue are not good.

Unfortunately, however, the language barrier between Americans and Japanese is minor when compared to cultural barriers. Everybody has different ways of expressing himself, and the content of one's message can differ radically even if the words are the same. Methods of communication also differ. Some cultures, like that of the United States, communicate primarily through words and willingly allow a very broad range of personal matters to be discussed publicly. However, members from a nearly opposite culture, like Japan, may stress nonverbal or intuitive communication and only permit a narrow range of personal matters to be aired publicly. Even simple communication between such contrasting cultures is difficult at best and at worst can lead to real problems.

Elements of the Japanese Personality:

While it is impossible to discuss the personality of any nation or people in a few pages, there are several distinct factors concerning the Japanese personality that should be explored. The bedrock principles that dominate Japanese culture are bound up in a number of words which refer to a series of interrelated values, motivations, attitudes, and practices that form the foundation of Japanese manners and ethics in business.[2]

The first of these words is *amae* which is often loosely translated as "indulgent love." It is the kind of clinging and dependent love that an infant might have for its mother. To a great extent, *amae* is a clinging relationship, a strong dependence on the trust and indulgence of another. The Japanese often desire a feeling of complete trust and confidence where they assume that they can rely on the indulgence of others. Within Japanese culture the strongest leader is one who encourages dependence (*amae*) among his colleagues and who, in turn, depends on those below him. Such a leader is unlikely to mislead employees because he would be hurting himself.

Another essential ingredient of a relationship with many Japanese is *shinyo* -- trust, confidence, or faith. Japanese are most reluctant to deal closely with people lacking *shinyo*. A person in whom Japanese have *shinyo* is a man of honor who will do what is expected of him whatever the cost. The development of *shinyo* comes only after a successful *amae* relationship has been established and thus may take many months or several years to develop. It means developing a close rapport with a Japanese and knowing what role to play within the relationship at a given point. A failure to follow the rules of *amae* or *shinyo* can lead to feelings of great resentment or hostility.

Where there is a lack of *amae* and *shinyo* in a relationship, one often sees *enryo*, which means consideration of things from a distance. This means not getting close to another party, to be polite but not to develop a long-term relationship or to do much business with that party. It is a feeling of some hostility and coldness. The Japanese feel constrained to practice this feeling of *enryo* because there are so often barriers between people who do not have an indulgent *amae* relationship. The Japanese tend either to ignore strangers and the outside world or to maintain a hostile stance toward them because the ability of Japanese to feel and to practice amae is based on long-term, close, interpersonal relationships.

It is possible to visualize the differences between the American and Japanese personality by drawing two sets of concentric circles. The American circle has a thin outer core and a large very solid inner core. The Japanese circle has a very hard and solid outer core and a small soft inner core.

The circle symbolizing Americans presents a clear portrait of the American character. Americans are very open people on a superficial level. People sharing a seat on a train or bus may enter into lengthy discussions with each other in which they readily give such information as their destination and domicile, their line of work, their marital status, political views, and the like. Americans like to move to a first-name basis as quickly as possible.3 Americans find it easy to do business with a wide range of people; the signing of contracts creates an intimate bond that is lacking in the relationships. There is, however, a solid core of intimate information that Americans will not give out to anybody except, perhaps, to close friends and family members. Traditionally such information includes one's salary, financial net worth, weight, sexual feelings and/or fantasies, and so on. An angry response would be elicited if one walked up to an older colleague and said, "Hello, Mary, how much do you weigh?" or "What is your average monthly salary?"

The Japanese, however, appear to be most reluctant to give out much, if any, information about themselves to casual strangers. Unless one is a part of a person's "uchi" (family or group), Japanese erect imposing barriers around their personalities that are very difficult to penetrate. When a

Japanese meets a stranger, he will talk about such safe subjects as the weather to avoid any chance of an embarrassing situation that might arise from the accidental revelation of private information. Once a relationship has developed to the point of trust and/or some intimacy, however, it is possible to penetrate the barrier. Once this critical step is accomplished, then the Japanese will reveal a vast amount of information.[4]

Thus, students of American and Japanese methods of communication find that the portion of the self that is shared with others, the public self, differs greatly between Americans and Japanese. Japanese prefer social encounters in which the extent of thought and feelings shared with others is relatively limited. The Japanese, in other words, are relatively repressed, private people who try not to expose too much of their private lives to public scrutiny. They prefer carefully regulated and predictable forms of conversation dealing with general topics in a somewhat superficial manner, while heart to heart conversations are left to the best of friends. Nonverbal communication, such as touch, is also limited except between Japanese who have broken through the barriers surrounding their respective personalities. It is for that reason that Japanese traditionally have bowed when meeting one another.[5]

While the Japanese veils himself in an atmosphere of secrecy even when there is nothing to hide, Americans appear to express themselves across a wider spectrum of topics at a significantly deeper and more personal level. They prefer spontaneous and detailed forms of conversation and, when confronted with a major problem, prefer assertive and expressive means of defense while Japanese, in keeping with the more guarded view of the self, prefer more passive forms of defense that tend to reduce involvement. Americans like to tell the world about themselves verbally and through touch; they are uneasy if they feel a person is trying to hide something. Many Japanese, on the other hand, have an innate terror of exposing their souls to public view and thus shy away from confrontations where the inner self can be exposed.

Politics reflect the inherent differences between Americans and Japanese. Americans like to expose their problems to public view. The misdeeds of the Nixon administration and Senator Gary Hart's friendship with Donna Rice became public morality shows, as did the infamous "Iranscam" of the Reagan administration of 1986-87. The Japanese have their share of public scandals that come into public view, but they do not stage seemingly endless public morality shows.

Consequently, it is clear why verbal communication is more important to Americans than Japanese. Words and other outward forms of communication mean a lot to Americans while Japanese seem to prefer more nonverbal and intuitive ways of making themselves understood. This is why Japanese value ritual and tradition, as well as etiquette, far more than Americans; custom tells the Japanese how they must behave and what they must say and do under given circumstances.

The Group in Japanese Society:

One of the more frustrating experiences of American executives in Japan is trying to get a direct answer from their Japanese counterparts. The Japanese host is not being rude or sneaky; he cannot speak on behalf of his company without consulting company officials and coming up with a group decision. An individual does not speak on behalf of the group without making sure that he has the backing of the group. Therefore, individual decision-making in Japan is rare.

There is the perhaps apocryphal story of the famous major league baseball slugger in Japan who had already hit four home runs for his team, the Tokyo Giants. The individual record for home runs in a game in Japan, as in the United States, is four and the slugger had a fifth chance at bat. The whole stadium waited with anticipation to see if their hero would hit a fifth homer, but everybody in the stadium was stunned to hear that the batter had taken himself out of the game and was being replaced by an inexperienced rookie who normally did not play. There are apparently two morals to this story. First, the slugger did not want to pin glory on himself; in Japan one is a hero when the company as a whole succeeds. The other moral is that it takes the skill and experience of all team members for ultimate success. By letting the young rookie into the game, the star was in fact strengthening the long-term prospects of the team.

While there is a strong streak of individualism in Japanese society, the group-oriented nature of Japanese culture is predominant. Japanese are much more likely to operate in groups than are Westerners. Where many Westerners stress some degree of individuality or independence in their conduct, many Japanese are quite content to conform in terms of dress, style and conduct.[6]

While the nuclear family is important today in both Tokyo and New York, extra-family groupings are much more important to the Japanese than to Americans. Today one is or is not within a certain *"uchi"* (meaning "within" in Japanese) or grouping where the barriers surrounding the Japanese personality are broken. Japanese will be close or intimate with those people within the confines of the *"uchi"* but will practice a certain degree of *enryo*, or distance, between non-*uchi* members.

Japanese society is divided into small cohesive groups which serve as the basis of a person's social and working life. Belonging to a group is essential to a person's happiness, security, and well-being. The same group extends into one's business and social life. Much of what goes on in Japan, including family relations, the decision-making process, and the structure of large corporations, revolves around the group structure of the society. In fact, it is difficult to function in Japan unless one belongs to a readily identifiable group. In many cases a person's group is based on his place of employment. Most of his friends will be fellow workers and will help in times of difficulty. His family will generally interact with other families of that particular group.

There is little interaction between members of different groups. One rarely associates with one's neighbors if they are not group members. As a result, there is little sense of community or neighborliness in urban areas of Japan. For examples, housewives rarely drop over to welcome a new neighbor. This makes life very lonely and hard for people who move into a new community and who do not belong to a functioning group. It makes life even more lonely and difficult for foreigners who reside in Japan because they rarely, if ever, can fit into a true Japanese group. On occasion an American will make close friends with a Japanese individual or family, but that is not easily done.

This group emphasis has greatly affected the whole style of interpersonal relationships in Japan. There is far more appreciation for a group player than for an individual star, and team spirit is more highly revered than individual ambition. Unlike the average American, a Japanese will not seek to emphasize his originality and independence. Rather, it is his willingness and ability to work for the team that counts. There is an old saying in Japan that the nail that sticks out will get banged down. Whereas Americans admire personal drive, some degree of forcefulness, and individual self-assertion, the Japanese give preference to operativeness, reasonableness, and understanding of others:

> The key Japanese value is harmony, which they seek to achieve by a subtle process of mutual understanding, almost by intuition, rather than by a sharp analysis of conflicting views or by clear-cut decisions, whether made by one-man dictates or majority votes. Decisions, they feel, should not be left up to any one man, but should be arrived at by consultations and committee work. Consensus is the goal -- a general agreement as to the sense of the meeting, to which no one continues to hold strong objections. One-man decrees, regardless of that man's authority, are resented, and even close majority decisions by vote leave the Japanese unsatisfied.[7]

The Japanese have found it necessary to avoid open confrontations in order to operate their system successfully. Consequently, in order to keep group harmony, each person involved in a negotiation process feels his way cautiously, only exposing his views as he sees how others will react to them. Much is suggested by implication. Thus, it is critical that no member be put into an embarrassing situation, which can occur when a clear "yes" or "no" answer is required. If a "no" answer is going to cause embarrassment or trouble for the other party, the Japanese will be very reluctant to give a sharp answer. What will come is a period of silence where no answer is given. In many circumstances this silence -- a clear example of the Japanese use of nonverbal communication -- is meant as a signal that a favorable response is not forthcoming.

Leadership in the group and in Japanese society as a whole is based more on seniority and length of experience than on raw ability (although ability does count for something, especially in getting a good education and job). Of course, the fact that a person has seniority does not necessarily make him a good leader, but, then, the role of leaders in Japan is different than in the United States. In the Japanese group, the good leader is not necessarily one who is sharp, has done his homework well, and knows all the answers. One or more of these attributes might be important in Japan, but in most instances a good leader does not concern himself with the details; instead, he allows subordinates to handle them. A good Japanese chief will be able to relate to his followers, to listen and empathize with them, and, above all, to maintain harmony within the group. Followers are supposed to be loyal and to work hard under a leader's direction. Thus, the leader and his followers are bound together by a long-term system of mutual obligation. The relationship is highly personalized and embraces all facets of life.

The leader of a Japanese group is rarely the crucial decision-maker as he would be in the United States. Often decisions are made on a lower level and are forwarded up to the top for formal ratification. In cases where there are differences of opinion, suggestions may come from various factions or individuals. Pros and cons are discussed at length until a consensus decision is reached. An able leader will be able to influence the proposal to some extent, but the decision that he articulates will be the product of group consensus. This being the case, the leader does not have to sell the decision to his subordinates or persuade them to accept it, as they already have been involved in the decision-making process itself.

Implications for Americans

Americans working with Japanese must adapt themselves somewhat to the Japanese system. The American coming to Tokyo must not expect to make significant progress on his first outing. If his company is new to Japan and if he is seeking new contacts with a Japanese firm, he must realize that it may take six months to a year before significant progress will occur. The Japanese generally are reluctant to do business with people outside their circle, or *uchi*. As long as there is a feeling of *enryo* with an American, Japanese will lack the confidence or trust necessary to do business with him.

On his first trip, an American should go to Japan not expecting to get much business done. Rather, he should go bearing appropriate gifts and expecting to meet many members of the Japanese company (*kaisha*). If the trip goes well, he will meet the president or some other high ranking member of the kaisha, but much more time will be spent with middle-aged mid-level employees of the Japanese company. It is critical to note that middle-ranking bureaucrats are very powerful and most crucial decision-making starts and ends with them. Senior officials are important for ceremonial events, for greeting important guests, and for giving advice, but if an American is really committed to a successful business relationship, he must get to know the forty to fifty year-old bureaucrats who actually run the Japanese *kaisha*.

The American will find that a great amount of time is spent socializing with Japanese. This goes against the American precept that business must come before pleasure. In Japan a good time comes with business because it is through the pursuit of pleasure that Japanese feel that they can break down the barriers separating them from people who do not belong to their uchi. Thus, on any given evening in Shinjuku or other entertainment districts of Tokyo, one will find countless small bars filled with middle-aged businessmen who come to drink, talk to their friends, sing a few songs, and get soothing words from an attentive hostess who pours their drinks and lights their ever-present Mild-7 cigarettes. It is a relaxing, almost festive atmosphere where people literally and figuratively roll up their sleeves and reveal their true personalities. The Japanese firmly believe that when you drink, you expose your true personality. Your defenses are down and any inhibitions are dropped; therefore, any *enryo* is sharply reduced or eliminated. It is here where one begins to develop some degree of *shinyo*.

This entertainment is very expensive, but it is a price that the Japanese are willing to pay to get to know a stranger. Little, if any, entertainment is ever done at the home of a Japanese executive. Americans going to Tokyo must be prepared to drink or at least go to these establishments. To appear reluctant is both rude and inconsiderate.

With luck and time an American will develop a relationship of trust with his Japanese counterparts. When the Japanese visit his home company, they should beent entertained lavishly. This does not mean taking the Japanese down to the local tavern to get roaring drunk. A good meal at a fine restaurant, a visit to an American home, and attention to the finer details of the Japanese's visit would serve as well.

Negotiating:

When negotiators meet at a bargaining table, they bring much more than briefcases full of notes and background papers. Integral parts of their baggage are their personalities and the rules and assumptions of the cultures that have shaped them. These differences raise fundamental questions: How is the bargaining to proceed? In what manner are positions to be presented? What sort of expectations will accompany them? It is possible to construct a model which will clearly delineate differences in methods of negotiating between Americans and Japanese.

One very frustrating factor for Americans dealing with Japanese culture is the fundamental fact that much of what makes up Japanese society is virtually the direct opposite of American custom. For example, while Americans like clear statements and relish direct confrontations, Japanese try to shy away from confrontations and strive for a degree of vagueness where nobody will be hurt and where there will be no losers or winners. Hence, if an American approaches a negotiation session with a Japanese, he can expect some rather contrary behavior from his counterpart. If the American were to reverse his tactics and mindframe, he might begin to appreciate the Japanese frame of mind.

Professor Mushakoji Kinhide, former Rector of the United Nations University in Japan, has constructed a workable model to study problems in negotiating between American and Japanese adversaries.[9] The problem, he notes, stems from the fact that the United States has a "choice" (*erabi*) type of culture which is diametrically opposed to and incompatible with Japan's "consensus" (*awase*) type of culture. Americans with their "choice" culture have a tendency to see the world in terms of a dichotomy -- big versus small, hot versus cold, and so on. They cannot tolerate continued vagueness or uncertainty; Americans want speakers to stop rambling on and to get to the point. The person who clearly states the "bottomline" is most appreciated. Thus, many successful Americans like to create intricate plans which they will attempt to follow with great precision. When Americans come to the negotiating table, they are inclined to present a firm set of demands and fully expect to leave with a clear set of principles that all parties to the talks will follow to the letter.

Negotiators facing each other in the United States often have an adversary relationship. A union on strike at an American company will approach management with a list of demands while management will come up with its own position paper. Each side will then bargain with the other trying to win as many concessions as possible. Of course, there is usually a compromise at the end, but American s are always asking who got the most from a new contract settlement. In other words, in a negotiation process in the United States, there are often winners and losers. If management got the best of the workers,there is often a feeling of distrust or disgust for management among the other employees.

Japanese consensus culture, on the other hand, rejects the idea that man can manipulate the environment and assumes instead that he must adjust himself to it. According to this way of thinking, the environment is not characterized by dichotomous concepts such as hot and cold. Rather, something may be rather cool or a bit warm, fairly sweet or fairly unsweet, rather large or somewhat small. In other words, the environment consists of a constantly changing continuum of fine gradations. "Consensus" is the logic of seeking to apprehend and adapt to these fine gradations of change.

Thus, when Japanese negotiate among themselves, they do not stake out their full positions at once. They may bring up a point to find out the other party's reaction and then the second party might bring up a point. Negotiations move slowly as each party seeks out the opinion of the other in order to work out a consensus agreement. Negotiations may go on for a very long time and might break down, but agreements when reached are mutually acceptable and there is rarely much, if any, rancor between the two parties. The Japanese use this same approach when dealing with Americans. Hence, when Japanese are negotiating with Americans, they are usually only willing to draw up a set of general principles that allow for future variations as circumstances change. This approach is, of course, very vexing for Americans who wish to formulate detailed and clearly labeled agreements with the Japanese.

The Negotiation Process Itself:

American psychologists specializing in the study of American negotiation techniques generally assume that the first stage of negotiation must be the defining of the issue at hand: talks can only begin when all parties know what sort of "view" to expect. Each party must place all of its main demands on the table at the very start. Negotiations cannot begin without this framing of the problem. This is not necessarily true in a "consensus" culture, however. Japanese do not want to begin a negotiation process where there are preconditions and preconceptions.[10]

There is also a very fundamental difference between Americans and Japanese concerning the matter of how the negotiations are to proceed. The American assumes that negotiations will go via a clear statement of position by each side while the Japanese preference is to infer the others' position without a clear explanation or statement of purpose. The Japanese expect the other party to sympathize with their position and to work toward an agreement that will also take the Japanese point of view into consideration. Hence, the Japanese feeling is, "You adjust to my position, and I'll adjust to yours."

Both the "choice" and the "consensus" approaches have certain advantages and disadvantages. A dimension in which the "choice" pattern is superior to "consensus" is that of autonomy and planning. Since the choice approach develops from an affirmation of the negotiator's individual standpoint, it is autonomous and independent, and since the "choice" negotiator is prepared to adopt the strategy which will maximize his own interests, he is able to devise a rational plan from the very start. The "consensus" approach, on the other hand, can, if mismanaged, lead one to drift passively along with the prevailing currents. Of course, the consensus negotiator has the distinct advantage of encouraging the other party to adapt as well, but when faced with a party that has an autonomous "choice" plan, he loses his advantage. The "consensus" approach, however, allows one to take into account the difference between theory and changing conditions. Since it does not require a clear statement of position, it leaves ample latitude for constant reinterpretations of one's stand.

Clues for the American Negotiator:

The goals and objectives of Americans and Japanese are totally different. The Japanese are interested in long-term investments while Americans look at each quarter. Thus, even when Japanese make decisions today, they are not making them for today's bottom line profit. They are thinking of future gain. According to Sondra Snowdon, a specialist in international protocol and in negotiating with the Japanese:

> The Japanese will never say no, because, to their thinking, everything is possible, if not at this hour, perhaps next year; if not in our lifetime, perhaps in somebody else's lifetime. But the Japanese will give clues that the deal isn't advancing, such as going back to the stage in the negotiations where you were six months ago. Be prepared for long periods of silence in Japanese business meetings. Americans who feel uncomfortable with gaps in the conversation and try to fill them will give away too much. Silence does not mean it is your turn to make a concession. Often, issues are discussed simultaneously, with no agreement until the end. This differs from the US tactic of discussing issues sequentially. A lack of response may only mean that the Japanese are considering your proposal very seriously.[11]

Snowdon suggests that when planning to negotiate with the Japanese, an American company should arrange a third party introduction. The company should send two, three or four people as a negotiating team and include a high-ranking executive in the first meeting. Bilingual business cards should be exchanged at the beginning rather than at the end, and when receiving a card (*meishi*) from a Japanese, each American should look it over with care. Failure to do so is very rude because it convinces the Japanese that Americans do not care about them. Americans must avoid the impression that they are in a hurry because of the Japanese need to build up trust. As negotiations proceed, always send the same representatives. Otherwise, the acquaintance period will begin again from scratch. Above all, Americans must avoid high-pressure sales techniques.[12]

Snowdon notes that there are four critical stages in negotiating:

> There is the prebusiness acquaintance stage of polite conversation. Next is the information stage where both sides find out about each other's needs, preferences and possibilities.

The persuasion stage follows when the Americans present their case and try to win over the Japanese delegation. In the final concessions and agreement stage the negotiations are concluded, using bargaining, compromise, or consensus.

The American negotiator tends to pass quickly through stages one and two and concentrates on persuasion. The Japanese, however, place great emphasis on stages one and two as a part of developing trust. Stage 2 is particularly important as the Japanese do not begin a negotiation with a goal in mind as do most American negotiators, but approach the negotiation with an open mind to determine the possibilities. In the final phase, the decision from the Japanese comes after a long period of consensus among themselves. They do not like bargaining and avoid confrontation at all costs.[13]

According to Snowdon, Americans and Japanese also have very different views on the bargaining process.

Americans tend to set high enough prices to allow for compromising and splitting the difference. Americans tend to negotiate price upfront; the Japanese prefer to leave price until the end. The first offer of the Japanese is usually close to the price they wish to pay. They do not like haggling and bargaining over price. It makes them lose face. Compromise, to the Japanese, implies they have lost something.[14]

Contracts:

The final stage of negotiating leading to an agreement or contract can cause grave problems. There are subtle but key differences in each nation's view of what a contract is supposed to be. Americans, for example, have at times accused Japanese of thinking nothing of breaking the terms of a contract or treaty. This problem stems from the fact that Americans view contracts as the "final choice" of the parties and that the terms of the contracts are absolutely binding on all parties.

Japanese, however, do not always share this view of contracts -- or at least the finer details of a complex agreement. To them, a contract is just one manifestation of the close consensus relationship between parties. Consensus relationships allow the principles to continue to make exceptions for each other, and the successful conclusion of one contract can encourage both parties to continue to seek further mutually beneficial concessions in certain conditions. Also, the Japanese, with their penchant for flexibility, have been known to seek changes in some of the strict provisions of a contract to meet some sudden changes in the relationship, such as a sudden revaluation of the yen. Both sides are supposed to benefit from this renegotiation process. The fact that Americans are so inflexible and unrealistic is a constant source of irritation for the Japanese. Akio Morita, one of the founders of Sony, states that when he first tried to market Sony products in American stores, there was a "real perception gap":

> We had to translate all of our contracts into English and explain the company on paper in minute detail. The first thing that puzzled the (American) lawyers and accountants was that many of our contracts specified that if, during the life of the contract, conditions changed in a way that affected the ability of either side to comply with the terms, both sides would sit down and discuss the situation. This kind of clause is common in Japanese contracts, and many companies do much or even most of their business without any contracts at all. However, it looked alarming to people who did not understand the way Japanese business is conducted in Japan. I guess this was the first real perception gap we came up against. The American side could not understand how we could sit down together and talk in good faith if the two parties were having a major disagreement.[15]

When Americans sign contracts, it is usually for a fixed period after which negotiations must resume. If company A has a 90 day contract with company B, but sees that a more beneficial relationship can be made by working with company C once the 90 days are over, many Americans would not hesitate to start a new relationship with company C. Much depends on the deal one can get with B or C. Japanese executives complain that signing a standard American contract is like reading an obituary -- it signals the end of a relationship. One agrees to a 90-day contract after which the relationship is officially over. A new contract must be negotiated.

The Japanese prefer enduring relationships. They like "evergreen clauses" that automatically extend them or which allow the contracts to continue while both parties negotiate in good faith. Frank Gibney, an American businessman with a great deal of business experience in Tokyo, explains the Japanese preference for consultations:

"Japan," wrote Yamamoto Shichihei in The Spirit of
Japanese Captialism, "is a society of 'consultation' (*hanashi-ai*)
whereas American and Europe represent societies of
'contract'....
the word for contract (*keiyaku*) may exist in Japanese,
but in meaning and content it is completely different from the
use of contract elsewhere." To the Japanese an agreement is
the result of consultation and the prelude to more consultation.
A contract can thus be readily changed by consultation, when
both parties sit down to review the progress of their
association.[16]

In Japan a verbal agreement between two trusting friends has as
much, if not more, weight than a written statement. A handshake and verbal
promise carry great weight in Japan. According to Gibney:

A Japanese company tends to think of a contract as the
beginning of a relationship, in which the terms change more
readily than the commitment. When the Japanese company
wants to change the contract, it first sends an emissary to the
party of the second part to begin discussions about a change.
A clause to the effect that "Both parties will set out to hold
discussions in good faith" -- on any revisions or disputed points,
is a staple of Japanese contract making. By and large the
contract...is regarded as merely the seal of an agreement
between the two parties, based on circumstances existing at the
time of their agreement.[17]

Thus, a contract with a Japanese firm is a secondary feature to a close
partnership that will endure for a long time. It is good etiquette in Japan
when signing a contract NOT to read it with care or to have lawyers present.
Such actions indicate to the Japanese that you do not trust their honesty and
integrity.

This does not mean that one must always adopt Japanese methods
when doing business with the Japanese. The type of negotiations and
contracts one will encounter will differ case by case, and it would be prudent
to learn as much as one can about one's Japanese counterpart before
proceeding.

CHAPTER II - NOTES

1.   My students are able to say far more after a term of Japanese than they can say in French or Spanish after a similar period of time.

2.   For an excellent discussion on these terms, see Boye DeMente, *The Japanese Way of Doing Business* (Englewood, New Jersey:Prentice Hall, 1981), pp. 13-14.

3.   Recently a car salesman began a discussion of the merits of his cars by saying, "Dan, call me Jack."
       I had only known Jack for five minutes, but we were already calling each other by our familiar names.

4.   Some of my closest Japanese friends think nothing of asking how much I paid for my new house or how much I weigh, and they give very detailed accounts of their marriages, friendships, and the like. It is at this stage that an *amae* relationship begins based on mutual *shinryo* or trust.

5.   A close Japanese friend still speaks with trepidation of the time he visited my in-laws' home near Boston and was suddenly hugged and kissed by an older female Italian. Italians may love to hug and kiss strangers, but it sends shivers up the spine of many traditional Japanese.

6.   Edwin Reischauer, *The Japanese* (Cambridge: Harvard. 1977), p. 129.

7.   Ibid., p. 135.

8.   For example, a visit to a discotheque with a Japanese businessman in early 1986 cost him about $105 for about 90 minutes. We got a small table, a hostess for each of us, all the alcohol we could drink, the right to dance with the hostess on the floor, and an opportunity to watch a harmless stage show.

9.   Mushakoji Kinhide, "Nihon bunka to Nihon Gaiko," in *Kokusai seiji to Nihon* (Tokyo: 1967), pp. 155-74.

10.   Ibid.

11.   Sondra Snowdon, "How to Negotiate with the Japanese," in *U.S. News and World Report* (September 28, 1987), p. BC-10.

12.   Ibid.

13.   Ibid.

14.   Ibid.

15.   Morita, *Made in Japan*, pp. 104-105.

16.   Frank Gibney, *Miracle by Design: The Real Reasons Behind Japan's Economic Success* (New York: Times Books, 1982), p. 120.

17.   Ibid., p. 122.

CHAPTER III

THE CULTURE OF JAPANESE MANAGEMENT

There exists a massive literature on the mystique of Japanese management, and some writers have suggested that the methods of Japanese managers need to be applied to corporations in the West if they are to do as well as the Japanese.[1] This is certainly a debatable point. Japan's management system was developed to meet the particular needs of Japanese society; and what works well in a group-oriented society may not suit a large company in New York. For example, it is doubtful that Japan's stable life-employment system would lend itself to a mobile society like that of the United States. Nevertheless, it is essential that Americans have some understanding of the Japanese system and an appreciation of efforts to import elements of the Japanese system into the United States by Japanese managers.

One cannot begin a discussion of management without noting again the dual structure of the Japanese economy. At the top are the large corporations, or *kaisha*, that are the flagships of the economy. They provide their workers with excellent salaries and working conditions and guarantee them lifetime employment. These companies and the people who work for them are the business elite of Japan. A career with one of these firms is the dream of many young men in Japan, but only a select few get the good jobs. Qualification for employment is limited to those people who graduate from the top thirty or so colleges and universities in Japan.

Those students who do not get into the most highly rated colleges do not usually get the chance to work for the big firms. Instead, they attempt to secure positions in small and medium-sized firms that cannot offer the high salaries, good working conditions, job security, and, most importantly, the prestige that comes with a position in one of the giant *kaisha*. Thus, the quality of education and, more importantly, the college that one graduates from, play the decisive role in one's career.

Education:

Japan is among the most upwardly mobile societies in the world. Beyond such obvious personal qualities as honesty and a sense of conformity, the sole criterion for an excellent position with a big firm is education. Japan has an excellent public educational system at all levels. Some of the finest colleges and universities are publicly supported, so the cost of a college education is very low by American standards. Entry into these colleges is open to any qualified student regardless of one's economic or social background. Japan has become a meritocracy.

There are two categories of elite universities: the top six that include such famous universities as Tokyo, Waseda, Kyoto, and Keio, and a secondary list which includes the top six and about twenty other schools such as Doshisha University in Kyoto. Tokyo University (Todai) is by far the most prestigious. The most famous department at Todai is the Hogakubu (Faculty of Law). A high percentage of Japan's business and political elite come from the Hogakubu. Many of the students I met while studying in the Hogakubu at Todai from 1975-77 will eventually become members of the Cabinet, heads of the top bureaucracies, and business leaders by the late 1990s.[2]

Since entry into a good managerial career depends so very much on education, Japan's educational system becomes extremely competitive at a very early age. To get the best training for the entrance examinations for these top universities, it is necessary to get into an excellent high school, many of which have their own sets of entrance exams. To get into a good high school, studying at a top junior high school is a major plus. Thus, it is critical to get into a good elementary school and there are even entrance exams for some of the better kindergartens.

Japanese students work much longer and harder than their American counterparts. The school year itself is fifteen days longer in Japan than in the United States. More importantly, the crucial difference between American and Japanese schools is an efficient use of time. Due to better order and discipline in Japan, Japanese students actually spend about a third more time learning during each class period than students in the United States.[3]

The Japanese digest a tremendous amount of information and do very well in such areas as science and math. In Japan, 95 percent of high school students graduate from high school compared to about 75 percent in the United States. In such areas as math, the best American high school students are barely able to reach the level of the average Japanese.[4] One gets similar results from Asian-American students in the United States.[5]

The importance of a good education is evident when one realizes that large Japanese corporations today are now managed by professional managers rather than by people who move into management because of family ownership of a firm. Thus, entry into a managerial career is based to a great extent on education rather than ownership or family connections. A recent study of 1,500 executives of major Japanese enterprises revealed that only 6 percent of those polled got their positions through ownership while the remainder got their posts by other means. Thus, a college education has become essential for a successful business career. Of the 1,500 executives samples, a rousing 90 percent had college degrees or the direct equivalent. To under-score the importance of the six major universities discussed above, as many as 60 percent of these men (there are very few high ranking female executives even now) had graduated from one of the top six universities.[6]

Very few Japanese go on to graduate school, and graduate training in business per se is rare. There are very few business school programs in Japan as compared to the United States. The companies do all of the training and show a strong preference for a young man who can be trained their way. They are not terribly interested in a person whose attitudes and work habits were shaped elsewhere.

When promising young men are preparing to graduate from college, the difficult task of trying to find a suitable company begins. It is not an easy search: there are only a few spots in the best government ministries, and quite often entry into a good firm is by competitive examination.

Lifetime Employment:

One of the prominent features of Japanese management is the practice of lifetime employment (*shushin koyo*) which is akin to tenure at an American college. The roots of Japan's lifetime employment system go back in Japanese history to a tradition of paternalism among small Japanese companies and merchant houses that grew in the seventeenth century.

The current system began early this century when bigger companies sought ways to reduce the costs that come with great labor mobility. There was also the challenge from an increasingly popular labor movement which encouraged these companies to extend the promise of job security as a way to discourage the rise of unions. Constant labor shortages before World War II also encouraged the companies to devise means to keep workers. Today a company generally guarantees its workers permanent job security and seniority-based wages and promotions. Workers are represented by company unions rather than by industry-wide unions.

Shushin koyo covers about 15 percent of the work force--those who work for the big *kaisha*. High school and college graduates must take exams given by each corporation. The few who get these coveted jobs often start with low salaries, but there are guaranteed annual promotions and pay hikes. Wages and promotion are based strictly on seniority. The average retirement age in Japan is now about sixty, at which point the worker must find other work to support himself.

Once a Japanese obtains a job with a *kaisha* and survives a six month probationary period, he is in for life. Management trainees, traditionally nearly all of whom have been men, are recruited directly from colleges when they graduate in the late winter of every year and are expected to stay with the companies for their entire working careers. In the large corporations there is little or no inter-company mobility. Unlike an American, who will often change jobs in his career, the Japanese worker on a lifetime plan would be regarded as a traitor if he abandoned his company in favor of another.

Dismissal does not come easily. In the British movie, *Educating Rita*, Rita, a student, asks her professor on what grounds he could be dismissed by his university. He replied, "Rape, but only rape on a grand scale." One might say nearly the same thing about Japanese corporations. One is not fired for any reason short of very serious moral misconduct. Poor performance or even incompetence is not grounds for dismissal.

The practice of lifetime employment has several very serious implications.[7] Since employees will stay with the same company for the balance of their working career, the choice of who will work for a firm is an extremely important matter. It is also a crucial decision for the college graduate, because a choice, once made, cannot be reversed.[8]

A major characteristic of the life employment system is the fact that one is hired as a generalist, not as a specialist for a specific position. When one enters a Japanese corporation, there is a long training period when the new employee will spend up to six months or a year in various offices or divisions of the company. Japanese tend to work as teams and a team may have various tasks over the course of a year. One way that a Japanese company can be productive and efficient is to have multi-talented workers who can perform a variety of tasks; managers from all over the company can at any given moment rush in to help the accounting department through a crisis, work with the international division in planning a trade agreement, and work with the public relations office to solve a company image problem.

Thus, when a new worker is employed, a particular skill or know-how is not required; rather,the individual's intelligence, educational background, and personal attitudes and attributes are closely examined. In essence, a company is like a family and is very careful to select only those people who will blend in well with the rest of the family--who will keep the peace and harmony. Oddballs are unwelcome. Thus, the backgrounds of many potential workers are carefully screened, often with the help of detective agencies.

Seniority:

Another unique aspect of Japanese management is the system of promotion and reward. The most important criterion is seniority, not personal ability or accomplishment. One's degree of seniority is determined largely by what year one entered the firm.

There is an annual "class" of recruits that come in each April after seniors graduate from high school, junior college, or a college/university. In 1986 an estimated 1.1 million workers appeared for their first day of work on April 1 in private firms and government offices throughout the country as the new fiscal year began.[9] Workers are largely identified by their class, and ties are usually closest among members of the same class.

Career progression is highly predictable and regulated. It is also very automatic. Members of a class usually start out with similar salaries and salary increases each year are uniform. The whole point is to maintain harmony within the group. To pay one person more than another within the same class, according to the theory of Japanese management, would cause stress, jealousy, and disharmony. What is important is not the status of the individual, but rather the overall success of the company. If all employees work hard and the company thrives, then everybody will benefit.

Individual evaluation, however, does occur. During the first half of one's thirty to forty-year career with a company, ability and real achievement are not immediately rewarded with significant raises in pay and authority. However, during the latter part of a person's career -- when he has reached the level of middle management -- a few people are selected for accelerated advancement and receive the small number of positions available in upper management. Promotion to the top ranks of management in Japan is very competitive and selective. Thus, a person with high career aspirations who desires perhaps a political career after retirement will start working very hard at a young age to impress his superiors. Very careful note is taken of talent, hard work, and dedication.

Early retirement for less successful workers is also an essential feature of the Japanese management system. Since only a few members of each class are selected for positions in top management and there must be room each year for members of younger classes to move up the hierarchy, it is critical that the less successful people in each class retire somewhere in their late fifties or early sixties.

Retirement does not necessarily mean a life of idleness. Poor pension benefits and a social security system that gives only limited funds to older people mean that many retired workers have to have some source of income. Many retirees from a large firm might work with one of the firm's smaller subsidiaries or might seek work elsewhere as a consultant or doing similar work for some other unrelated company. Thus, for example, when the state of Virginia was setting up an office in Tokyo to encourage Japanese investment and industry in the state, the man chosen to run the Virginia office was a recent retiree from the Bank of Tokyo, since he could establish critical links between Japanese businessmen and officials in Virginia. A few very successful businessmen might get high corporate positions elsewhere or a chance to enter politics.

Compensation is also based on the seniority system. A younger employee will make a fairly small salary, but he will accept it with the understanding that his pay will go up in regular increments and that by the time he nears retirement, he will be making a great deal of money. Increases in compensation are based on length of service, not on the quality of one's individual effort. Personal and group achievement are reflected in corporate success and profit, which leads to higher regular pay and bonuses for all employees.

Compensation consists of a wide variety of both tangible and intangible factors. In addition to cash benefits, which may seem low when compared to what an American doing the same job might earn, there is also an important range of fringe benefits which can make a Japanese firm's compensation package very attractive. These fringe benefits might include housing, vacation trips, good recreational facilities and, most importantly, the availability of low cost loans for such things as housing and a new car.

Actual pay consists of a monthly salary and a semi-annual bonus from the company that is often based on corporate profits. The monthly salary is generally fairly low by American standards, but one's annual pay is increased by as much as fifty percent with the bonus. There are at least a few job categories where younger Japanese are making more money that their American counterparts.[10]

Today, the challenges facing many large Japanese manufacturing firms, along with rapidly changing employment trends in Japan, threaten to challenge Japan's traditional system of lifetime employment. In the late 1980s, several large steel and other manufacturing corporations in Japan are having to lay off workers, including those who had entered the company with the assumption they had jobs for life. This is most discouraging and many people who had expected a comfortable retirement are suddenly out on the streets looking for new jobs. The numbers of such people are not great, but the very fact that established firms are letting go of workers with "tenure" tends to worry all other "tenured" workers.

Unions:

Another aspect of Japanese management is the company union. Unlike the United States where people work for craft or other specialized unions, in Japan all the employees of one company including those in management, join the union regardless of their skills or job category. The worker does not have a separate skill identification outside of the company, and the union does not exist as an entity separate from, or with an adversary relationship to, the company.[11]

This linking of the company with the worker puts severe limits on independent action from several unions because the worker does not wish to hurt or destroy the economic situation of his company. There are occasional strikes, but in general they are designed to strengthen the company as a whole rather than to increase workers' benefits.

Women in Management:

Although the status of women in Japan is rapidly rising, they are still second class citizens in the eyes of many of the traditional large Japanese corporations. A woman may work for a few years after graduation from junior college or college and then leave work to get married by her late twenties.[12]

Japanese firms publicly proclaim that they treat men and women equally in promotions. A survey conducted by Japan's Institute of Labor Administration in 1986, however, indicates that old practices still are in force. Only 1.2 percent of the 321 major companies surveyed had women in positions above the ranks of divisions managers.[13] Thus, although there are more women at work than men in Japan, women tend to hold temporary or part-time jobs with few, if any, of the benefits accorded to most men.

The situation, however, is not entirely hopeless for women. Some Japanese women find very rewarding careers working for foreign firms that are far less discriminatory in their attitudes towards women. Other women do very well in smaller companies. This is especially true with newer companies in such growth areas as computers where companies are both new and small - -and thus are not bound by tradition. Women play a vital role at all levels of the computer industry in Japan and many of Japan's computer programmers are women. Furthermore, even some of the older firms are breaking tradition and are permitting a few women to enter their managerial hierarchy. For example, in April 1986 the newly privatized Japan Tobacco, Inc. hired a woman among 35 new employees. It was the first time that this organization had hired a female college graduate in nineteen years.[14]

In 1986 a law was enacted in Japan which makes equal treatment of women in the workplace absolutely mandatory. The law has been hailed as a victory for women's equality in Japan, but the notion that men and women have identical rights goes against the traditional division of society and work by gender. Men and women have very different functions in Japanese society, and both must perform their duties to the utmost if the traditional society is to thrive.

Gender in Japan is a very important organizing category which creates a number of dual relationships in society. The most crucial of these dualities is that of home and work. Home is the center of the woman's life, while work is that of the man's. Many Japanese believe that this societal balance will be upset if there is any change in traditional male/female roles. If women were to work outside the home for any considerable period without providing maternal care for children, the children would not develop properly. For example, it is the mother who must play the crucial role of seeing to it that children are well educated so that they can succeed in Japan's highly competitive society. Furthermore, if women were to spend all of their time at work, shirking such basic responsibilities as cooking and cleaning, men would not eat or dress well. If men worked at home, they would not be able to devote full attention to work.[15] Most Japanese believe it takes the combined efforts of women at home and men at work for Japan to be prosperous.

In traditional Japan, gender categorization of society led to a dualistic situation where men and women had functions that were both opposite and complementary of each other. According to the traditional Chinese view of Yin and Yang, there are two forces which together make up a whole. They stand in opposition to each other as passive and productive forces, but the existence of one is mandatory for the survival of the other. In Japanese society the male gender represents the producer, who is both brave and aggressive. The female gender is, on the other hand, meant to be at home and to be both gentle and retiring. Each gender has its role: the men go out, work hard, and bring home the money; women stay at home, manage the money, take care of the family, and maintain their households. Thus, both sexes are separate but equal. The sexes are separated and are thus able to work in a very complementary fashion for the smooth functioning of society in Japan.[16]

Executive Managerial Style:

There are several aspects of Japanese managerial style and decision-making that differ markedly from the United States. They include the following: an emphasis on the flow of information and initiative from the bottom up, making top management a facilitator of decision-making rather than the source of authority and decisions; using middle management as both the impetus for and shaper of policy; stressing consensus as a way of arriving at decisions; and paying close attention to the well-being of workers.[17]

In the West authority is equated with positions of seniority. As a person moves up in rank, he often becomes increasingly isolated from the rest of the lower-ranking officers and staff. A company president might have a big office on the top floor where he can have privacy to plan and implement policy. In Japan, on the other hand, the top manager is not the sole decision-maker. Often, plans and decisions have already been made when he finally gets a copy of the final plan. The top manager's job is to find ways to maintain anatmosphere of harmony and accord within the company so that the others can work together. A Japanese chief-executive office (CEO) is a consensus builder, a harmonizer of people. This is as true in politics as inbusiness. Leading politicians are harmonizers, not dashing individualists, such as John F. Kennedy and Michael Dukakis.

American-style management emphasizes that three types of skills are required of a manager: technical, human, and conceptual. Top management requires primary conceptual skills, followed by human skills, and then technical skills (given only about 10 percent of total skills percentage). Middle managers must possess primarily human skills (50 percent) with equal amounts of conceptual (25 percent) and technical (25 percent) skills.

First-line superiors require primarily technical skills, followed by human skills with only about 10 percent conceptual skills needed.

Unlike its American counterpart, it seems that top management in Japan needs primarily human skills while middle managers require more conceptual skills to address decision making.[18] A senior manager in Japan plays a vital role as a facilitator in shaping proposals (human skills). He will listen to the comments and suggestions of subordinates and will, if necessary, raise questions and make appropriate comments. The subordinate will then go back and will act on those questions and suggestions. The key persons in the decision-making process are the middle managers. Unlike the United States where middle management might be the functional specialists who carry out their boss's directives, the Japanese counterpart not only must take the initiative to perceive problems and formulate tentative solutions, but he must also shape a comprehensive plan to meet the problem. Thus, if one is looking at the power-structure of a company in the United States, very often one must look towards the top of the organization; however, throughout Japanese history, it is those people at the middle levels in the bureaucratic machine who have had a real grip on the situation and who have actually implemented policy (conceptual skills). Various studies of Japanese domains during the Tokugawa period (1600-1867) demonstrate that real power was not in the hands of the *daimyo* or lord, but rather with lower - or middle - ranking *samurai* or retainers. This, then, is precisely the reason why a foreign visitor to a Japanese corporation will be introduced to and entertained by people in middle management positions.

Decision-Making:

It is very important to distinguish between the Western and Japanese concepts of decision-making. For a Westerner, moving towards a decision is arriving at an answer to a question. For the Japanese, on the other hand, the important element in decision-making is actually defining the question or getting all concerned to fully understand the problem; it is important to decide whether there is a need for some kind of decision and what the decision is about. Consensus comes when a question is defined -- what are we talking about? Why are we doing this? The Japanese agonize for a long time over what the decision is really about, not what the decision should be. Once this is accomplished, it usually does not take long to find an answer.

The essence of the group-decision style of management is the *ringisho* (literally, "decisions in a circle by document"). The whole process is quite similar to the system in the United States where staff officers, quite often at a junior level, work out major strategies which are then submitted to the commander, who often does little more than initial the document himself.[19] When a new idea is broached or a new policy is suggested, the formulation of the actual plans is assigned to some junior person or group on the planning staff or to a junior department head. When the plans are drawn up, they are passed from department head to department head up the managerial ladder to ensure agreement. There are also a great number of conferences, and many additions, deletions, and suggestions are amended on the document. Every person who agrees to the plan affixes his seal to the document. Ultimately, the document is presented to the managing director, who takes it to the president for his formal seal. The system is bottom-up in the sense that the need for a new decision or plan is often recognized by those at a lower level of the company, quite often by middle managers. The system is consistent with the group-orientation of Japanese society because people at all levels have some input into the system; those who are affected by the decision all participate in the decision-making process.

The Westerner often expresses impatience with the apparent cumbersomeness of the Japanese decision-making process. In the United States a CEO may confer with some of his subordinates before arriving at a decision, but, if necessary, he or she can move quickly on behalf of the whole company. Sometimes CEOs in the United States must then spend time selling and explaining the decision to the rest of the firm. If it is not a popular decision, the CEO may experience difficulty in getting the staff to implement the decision.

The Japanese, on the other hand, do not have to spend any time at all selling a decision or explaining it to others on the staff. Everybody has been involved in the decision-making process, and all complaints and signs of dissent have been handled. Once a decision is made, the Japanese can move with great speed to implement it. This is a form of "consensus management" that traditionally has been rarely successful in the United States, but some American corporations are making cautious attempts to improve participative management which would correspond to the Japanese approach.

The Godfather Concept:

One thing that many American workers complain about is management's lack of concern about their welfare. They sometimes feel that the company does not really care about their lives, which can lead to a sense ofalienation and isolation for the worker. In Japan, however, the traditional concept of the group, as well as the need for harmony and good reciprocal relations as stressed in Confucianism, requires a closer relationship among workers in any company.

One way to watch out for worker discontent is what Peter F. Drucker calls the "godfather" system of Japanese management.[20] Every younger employee is assigned a "godfather" who is a person in upper management who is supposed to keep a friendly eye on his "godson." The "godfather" is expected to know the young man, to see him on a frequent basis, to be readily available for advice and counsel, and to introduce him to the right bars and the like. If the young man is upset with some aspect of the company or if officials want to relay some message to him about his conduct, the "godfather" will act as a quiet and unofficial conduit of such information. The "godfather" will also make informal evaluations of his "godsons" to upper management because of his familiarity with these employees.

The "godfather" is usually a senior member of a firm chosen from the ranks of upper middle management for his sensitivity and candor. The "godfathers" are not the chosen few who at age 55 will become top management; rather, they are the most respected of the older staffers who will retire at age 55 or who will be shifted to one of the affiliate organizations. Therefore, they are unlikely to build factions of their own or to play internal politics. They are free to work with their far younger colleagues.[21]

Japanese Management in the United States:

Every year several new Japanese companies set up factories and/or offices in the United States. The Southeast has been especially successful in attracting Japanese industry in the mid-1980s with several large facilities being built in North Carolina, Kentucky, and Tennessee. Two major concerns of these firms have been how to handle the American worker and how to incorporate Japanese management into the American system.

The implementation of Japanese management can be quite subtle. One does not want to make the American worker think that he or she is working in an alien environment. The key is to try to improve the morale of the American worker by making him feel that management cares about him as an individual and that his work for the company is meaningful. Japanese managers try to elicit cooperation with Americans by presenting themselves as equals. At some plants there are no privileged parking lots for executives, all employees eat in the same cafeteria, executives have no separate offices, and everybody wears the same uniform. Many of these companies hold weekly meetings with as many employees as possible to get their input concerning the operation of the company.

American-based Japanese companies train their workers as generalists, as they do in Japan. Workers often work in teams that are given a variety of assignments. Since everybody does several jobs under the Japanese teamwork approach, work is spread more evenly. Thus, unlike some American companies where production can be stalled when one department is behind in its work, in Japanese-run corporations other teams can come to the rescue if production runs into a snag. In some companies there is a complaint box where workers are promised a very quick response to their problems.

Japanese firms do not offer lifetime employment to their American workers, but every effort is made not to fire workers, even under very difficult conditions. Employees may be moved around to different jobs within the company and wage increases may be blunted on occasion, but the company tries to make the worker feel that his job is secure and that his loyalty is highly valued. In at least several companies American workers feel no need for a union because they are convinced that the company does indeed care about them.

Japanese practices are not static and are under-going constant change. Although most of the practices described above can be found at a great many Japanese corporations, many firms will make specific modifications to meet their needs. For example, some companies are experimenting with methods of paying workers according to their productivity; using incentive pay will hopefully spur production. Another challenge to the current system concerns the heavy cost of pay to senior managers. Pay increases that are granted automatically with each additional year of service become very costly for the *kaisha* as seniority increases. Therefore, anumber of experiments are underway in various *kaisha* to somehow flatten the wage curve at an earlier point in a person's career. The rationale for this move is that family and other responsibilities grow less past the mid-forties and that a flattening of the wage increase need not work a hardship.[22]

CHAPTER III - NOTES

1.   One notable proponent of this view is William G. Ouchi. See his book, *Theory Z: How American Business Can Meet the Japanese Challenge* (Reading, MA: Addison-Wesley, 1981).

2.   Over half of Japan's postwar cabinet members are graduates of Tokyo University.

3.   "Memorizing vs. Thinking: Americans Study the Lessons of Japanese Schools," in *Newsweek* (January 12,1987) p. 60, and "The Brain Battle" in *US News & World Report* (19 January 1987) pp. 58-65. These articles discussed a 111-page report, "Japanese Education Today," issued in late 1986, by the U.S. Department of Education.

4.   Edward B. Fiske, "Japanese Education Fades at the Finish," in *The New York Times*, Sec. 4, p. 6, (11 January 1987).

5.   However, there are some definite drawbacks to the Japanese system. The entrance exams test one's knowledge of factual information. There is less evidence of individual creativity or analysis among the many Japanese students I have taught at American colleges. In the long run the much maligned American educational system may train one much better for a life of independent and original thought.

6.   *Encylopedia of Japan*, 1983 ed., s.v., "Japanese Management," by Michael Yoshino.

7.   *Ibid.*

8.   In the 1980s the system is showing signs of erosion, and a few talented managers are on occasion able to shift jobs. Several of my friends in Japan have made at least one key shift in their late twenties, but they had special talents, such as fluency in English, that made them especially appealing to companies that needed personnel that could manage offices in the United States. Teachers in various schools can more easily make shifts because of the need for good teachers.

9.   *The Japan Times* (19 April 1986), p. 2.

10. . This is certainly true in college teaching where my Japanese colleagues earn far more than my American colleagues who teach at both smaller colleges and universities.

11.   Abegglen and Stalk, p. 205.

12.   According to a Japanese executive who visited my college in 1985: "The notion that we fire women after they have been with us for a few years is not correct. To do so would be strictly against the law. However, it is very

true that we strongly encourage women to leave our employment when they get married and especially when they have children."

13.   "Firms Not Ready for Female Managers," *The Japan Times* (28 June 1986), p. 8.

14.   *Japan Times* (19 April 1986), p. 11.

15.   Nancy Rosenberger, "Japanese Women: Paradoxes of Power and Self." Paper presented at the Southeast Conference of the Association for Asian Studies Conference at Chattanooga, Tennesse 16 January 1987, pp. 1-2.

16.   *Ibid.*, p. 8.

17.   Richard Tanner Johnson and William G. Ouchi, "Made in America (Under Japanese Management)," in The Harvard Business Review, ed., *How Japan Works* (Cambridge, 1981),p. 36.

18.   Based on a memo from Gordon Hammock, Assistant Professor of Business Administration at Mary Baldwin College, January, 1988.

19.   Frank Gibney, *Miracle by Design: The Real Reasons Behind Japan's Economic Success* (New York: Times Books, 1982), p. 62.

20.   Peter F. Drucker, "What We Can learn from Japanese Management," in *Harvard Business Review*, p. 31.

21.   *Ibid.*

22.   Abegglen and Stalk, pp. 191-198.

CHAPTER IV

THE CHANGING NATURE OF THE OCCUPATIONAL STRUCTURE
OF THE JAPANESE ECONOMY

In the mid-1980s Japan finds itself on the threshold of a new age, the third since the Meiji Restoration of over a century ago. The first period, which encompassed most of Japan's history through the late nineteenth century, was dominated by agriculture. The second age -- urban industrialization -- has endured over the past century, but is now showing definite signs of coming to an end. Recently, Japan, like the United States, has entered into a post-industrial economy dominated by the production and manipulation of information and high technology manufacturing, operating within an increasingly global-scale framework of business interactions. Consequently, the Japanese are experiencing some fundamental dislocations, and Japan has its own "Rust Belt" of decaying factories and unemployed workers, though not on as large a scale as the U.S.

The once highly optimistic mood of Japanese business and government leaders in 1987 has turned to one of gloom and worry. While no serious student of the Japanese economy is predicting absolute doom and gloom, and while there is no doubt that Japan will remain a major economic power for the rest of this century, the growth rate of the Japanese economy, which at one point a generation ago regularly grew at a rate of ten percent or more a year, sank to 2.5 percent during 1986.[1] The Japanese economy in 1986 was badly battered by the rising yen, renewed competition from Taiwan and South Korea, a sixteen-percent decrease in exports, and a falling industrial production.

These changes have been accompanied by dramatic changes in the structure of Japan's economy and in the nature of its occupational structure as well. The following is a brief analysis of Japan's contemporary occupational structure, which includes the following three sectors:

        1) primary, or agriculture related work;

        2) secondary, or industry related employment;

        3) tertiary, or service related professions.

Primary Sector:

The primary sector includes that portion of the labor force engaged in agriculture, forestry and hunting, and fishing. This sector dominated the Japanese economy up through the 1940s; since then it has experienced a significant decline in relation to the secondary and tertiary sectors due to Japan's rapid postwar industrialization. In the 1870s primary industries accounted for 82.3 percent of the gainfully employed population of Japan, but employment in agriculture declined to about fifty percent at the end of World War II. Employment in the primary sector declined to about 4 percent in 1980 (See Chart 1).

There are many reasons for the decline of the primary sector. Few young people are becoming farmers or fishermen; this means that the average age of agricultural workers is rising and that the sector's labor force is becoming depleted through the retirement and death of workers. Furthermore, since the 1960s there has been a general decline in the forestry and fishing industries. Fishermen have been beset by increased international competition and pollution and by the depletion of domestic waters. For all of these reasons, seasonal and permanent migration to cities is increasing, resulting in a general drop in the rural population. Japan, like the United States, is becoming an increasingly urban nation.

By the mid-1980s Japan's agricultural sector has displayed three major characteristics: ultra-small-scale management, a concentration in the production of rice, and a growing socioeconomic transformation of farming families. The average farm holding averaged in size from 1-2 hectares (2.7-5.4 acres), but improvements in agricultural productivity has raised yields per hectare to levels that are among the highest in the world. The production of rice, still the all-important staple food of most Japanese, is more than sufficient to feed the entire nation. Improvements in farming techniques, including the introduction of highly efficient farming machinery and fertilizers, have greatly increased the per capita yield per farmer. This in turn has reduced the need for so many farmers and the amount of time and energy needed by each farmer to produce sufficient levels of rice.

More recently, farming has become a sideline occupation for many people -- especially older people. By the early 1980s many farmers were abandoning their traditional winter crops to work in urban areas, and a majority of farmers were supplementing their incomes by working on other jobs. Today, many of the people working on farms are men over the age of 60 and older married women.

The decline in traditional farming in rural areas has been partly counterbalanced by the rise of truck farming near some urban areas. The seasonal growing of green vegetables and the increased use of greenhouses have helped meet demands for these products in urban centers.

Despite its decline, the primary sector will continue to play an important role in the Japanese economy. Continued government protection of agriculture seems certain, especially since the Japanese do not want to become totally dependent on the outside world for all foods and because the conservative ruling Liberal-Democrats want to keep the farm vote. The government provides farmers with substantial subsidies and protection from the importation of agricultural goods since farmers' votes count more than those of urban dwellers due to carefully gerrymandered districts that are smaller in rural areas than in cities. Farmers, in turn, vote heavily for the Liberal-Democrats.

Chart 1: Employment composition by Sector-Japan:

	1955	1965	1977	Changes
Agriculture, Fish, etc.	40.2%	23.5%	11.9%	-28.3%
Manufacture & Mining	19.5%	24.9%	25.5%	+ 6.0%
Construction	4.4%	7.3%	9.2%	+ 4.8%
Transport/ Communication	4.7%	6.2%	6.9%	+ 2.2%
Utilities	31.2%	38.4%	46.3%	+15.1%

Source: Bureau of Statistics, Office of the Prime Minister, *The Labor Source Survey.* Quoted in Miyohei Shinohara, *Industrial Growth, Trade, and Dynamic Patterns in the Japanese Economy* (Tokyo: 1982).

Chart 2: Composition of National Income by Economic Activity, Japan (1970-1980) and Selected Industrial Countries (1980):

	Primary Industry	Secondary Industry	Tertiary Industry
Japan			
1970	7.8	38.1	54.1
1980	3.5	37.5	58.9
Italy	6.3	42.1	51.6
United Kingdom	1.8	39.3	58.8
West Germany	2.1	34.4	58.8
France	4.3	37.8	57.9
United States	2.7	31.5	65.7

Source: Bank of Japan, *Nihon keizai o chushin to suru hikaku tokei*, 1982, (comparative international statistics on the Japanese economy), (Tokyo: 1982), pp. 47ff as quoted in Martin Bronfenbrenner and Yasukichi Yasuba, "Economic Welfare," in Yamamura and Yasuba, *The Political Economy of Japan*, p. 109.

Secondary Sector:

Today the Japanese economy is still strongly influenced by heavy industries like automobiles, steel, shipbuilding, and chemicals. Indeed, it is the growth of the secondary sector, which includes that portion of the labor force engaged in manufacturing, construction, and mining, that has made Japan the economic superpower that it is today. Almost nonexistent in Japan until the late 19th century, this sector grew rapidly after 1900 and comprised 40 percent of the labor force in 1980.

Unlike many modern industrialized states where the secondary sector is expected to exceed the tertiary sector until a mature stage of industrialization is reached, Japan's secondary sector has always been smaller than the tertiary sector since the industrialization process started in the late nineteenth century. The secondary sector has experienced great, often explosive, growth since 1900, but it has always remained proportionally behind the service sector because Japan's historic labor surplus has forced many people to engage in unproductive work, resulting in considerable unemployment and very low pay.

Beginning with silk and cotton spinning and, later, various heavy industries, Japan's secondary sector experienced its first real growth after the first Sino-Japanese war (1894-95). Its share of the labor force grew from 20.6 percent in 1920 to 26.8 percent in 1940. The secondary sector suffered a temporary setback during and immediately after World War II because of a huge shift of manpower into the military and the destruction of Japanese factories by American bombers in 1944 and 1945, but employment in the sector returned to a quarter of the workforce by 1950 and to 35 percent in 1970. In the early 1950s there was a temporary flow from the tertiary to the secondary sector as workers moved from low-productivity service trades to larger, better paying jobs in industry. Later, after 1960, there began a continuous flow of workers from heavy industry back to the service industry, which had become much more modern and productive. Since the early 1970s there has also been a noticeable internal flow of manpower within the secondary sector from smaller low-productivity and low-wage firms to larger, more productive, and better paying firms.

The parts of the secondary sector experiencing the most growth since the early 1950s include the automobile, iron and steel, chemical, shipping, andelectronics industries. The only area that experienced great decline before 1980 was mining, particularly coal mining. The automobile, steel, shipbuilding, and electronics industries were the driving force behind Japan's tremendous economic expansion of the 1960s and 1970s.

In the late 1980s, however, there have been signs of real decline in certain parts of the secondary sector and rising unemployment among many industrial workers. In 1986 Japan's Economic Planning Agency reported that Japan's economy is heading for a real slump. It reported that domestic economic activity is slack and that bleak prospects also cloud the labor front, with overtime work and job vacancies on the decline and unemployment on the rise.[2] According to The Wall Street Journal, unemployment in Japan is becoming a major issue:

> Unemployment is becoming a hot issue in Japan, for the first time in many years. Nearly every day there is some

disturbing announcement about the loss of wages or jobs.
Shipbuilders are closing down yards.   Steel-makers are
experimenting with "rotational" layoffs. Japan's remaining coal
mines are closing. The weaker automakers are shunting
workers into obscure affiliates or turning them into car
dealers.[3]

In July of 1986 Japan's unemployment rate jumped to a postwar high of 2.9
percent. Even more ominous was the fact that the monthly total included
1.02 million men, or 3.1 percent of the male work force.[4] These rates
continued into 1987. The impact of the strong yen on imports and corporate
profits brought the rate up to 3.2 percent in May of 1987. In addition, the
number of overtime hours worked fell substantially below the norm in
manufacturing. There was expansion of employment in 1987 in the service
area; employment in the service area expanded by nearly 700,000 jobs in
1986 in contrast to a loss of 90,000 jobs in the manufacturing area and
140,000 in agriculture.[5]

The decline in employment in the manufacturing sector is expected to
continue in coming years in Japan. Due to the life employment system,
manufacturing firms have retained about one million redundant workers on
the payroll. Faced with continued competitive pressure posed by the high
yen, these firms must take strong measures in coming years to reduce labor
costs. The Ministry of Labor is even going so far as to predict that 2.2 million
jobs will be lost in the manufacturing sector due partly to increased overseas
production -- such as the making of Hondas in Ohio.[6]

Chart 3:International Comparison of Unemployment Rates:

	1985	1986	1987 (Jan.-March)
Japan	2.6%	2.8%	2.9%
USA	7.1%	6.9%	6.6%
West Germany	9.3%	9.0%	8.8%
France	10.1%	10.5%	10.9%
Britain	11.3%	11.6%	11.1%

Source: *Tokyo Financial Review*, June 1987.

For those people in the deteriorating industries, unemployment is a traumatic experience. Some of those workers losing their jobs were guaranteed lifetime employment and now they are being released. Thus, companies are losing face because of their need to break commitments, which goes against the very grain of the Japanese employment system.

The reason that the shipping, steel, mining, and other heavy industries have been declining for several years is in part because of severe competition from South Korea, Taiwan, and other developing countries. This competition has forced Japan to shift away from smokestack industries and toward high technology and services. According to Kazuo Tamiya, an analyst at a research institute in Tokyo, "The yen's depreciation is the critical factor. Without it, the changes would have happened more slowly."[7]

The steel industry has been the big loser recently. The five major steelmakers posted operating losses of several billion dollars and only averted a total collapse by selling undervalued assets, such as stock in other companies.[8] According to some estimates, Japan's steel industry could lose as much as $2.2 billion during the 1987 fiscal year. In early 1987 steelmakers announced plans to cut 40,000 jobs by 1990 and to shutdown six of the nation's 38 operating blast furnaces. Industry experts estimate that production could fall to 80 million tons in 1990 against a peak of 104 million tons in 1985, while exports will drop to half of 1985's 34 million tons. In addition to layoffs and cuts to save money, steel firms are investing in such areas as computer technology, construction, engineering, consulting, and new materials. One large steelproducer, Nippon Kokan, has developed a food company that raises pigs and produces ham and other meat products which could generate sales of up to $60 million in 1990.[9]

The future of the steel industry does not look bright. A report issued by the Ministry of International Trade and Industry (MITI) in March 1987 stated that there will be nearly 100,000 excess steel workers by 1990 and that steel production will drop to only 88 million tons by the early 1990s. It urged the six big steelmakers to cut their work force by 36 percent, or 96,000 employees, to save 680 billion yen in personnel expenses and thus maintain a profitable stance in the next decade.[10] Although their figures for 1990 may differ slightly, both industry and government analysts see grim times ahead for big steel in Japan.

Japan's once famous shipping industry is also on the verge of disappearing.   Due to South Korea's growing market share in ship production, Japan's 1990 output might be a third or less of the 9.3 million gross tons that made it the leading producer of ships in 1984.11

Japanese shipbuilders with diversified capacities, like Mitsubishi Heavy Industries, are making the transition into the growth world of high technology.   In 1985 Mitsubishi's growing aerospace division accounted for 15 percent of the company's sales.   The company is building F15 fighters under license from McDonnel Douglas for the Japanese military and is a prime contractor for Japan's nascent rocket program.   There are four other Japanese manufacturers that are working toward the development of sophisticated fighters and are hoping that the Japanese government will offer them contracts instead of purchasing these jets from abroad.[12] Thus, the key to the future success of these and other companies is diversification and penetration into the modern industries of the tertiary sector.

Japanese makers of consumer electronics, who until recently dominated world markets, are today being swamped by low-cost competitors. Such leading audio manufacturers as Aiwa, Akai, and Sanyo have cut their domestic staffs and have moved much of their manufacturing to Malaysia and other Southeast Asian states.   Even Matsushita, today the world's largest consumer electronics manufacturer, intends to move much of its production overseas in the early 1990s.[13]

Even Japan's vaunted automobile industry has had difficulties as car production dipped during the first quarter of 1987.   As in the shipping industry, Japanese auto makers are busy searching for higher value-added lines of business. The Toyota Motor Corporation has become interested in telecommunications, Nissan Motor Company has been designing satellite-mounted kickmotors, and Isuzu Motors is making pioneering efforts to develop ceramic technologies. Automobiles can be produced at lower cost in other Asian countries; therefore, some Japanese automakers are concentrating primarily on more expensive luxury cars. Nobody expects the major Japanese automakers to fall in the near future, but product diversification and increased involvement in high tech are necessary for future growth.

In the steel industry, as in the rest of the nation's companies, there is a major effort to hold down costs and avoid layoffs. In a recent survey the Labor Ministry in Tokyo found that 28 percent of Japanese companies had cut overtime, given workers longer holidays, or had transferred workers to other divisions or affiliated companies. Only one percent asked employees to retire on a volunteer basis.[14]

Most companies rely on an intricate network of relationships to absorb excess workers. According to this system, a large corporation will transfer employees to another often smaller company with which it has some special connection. Transferred workers generally get their full pay; the new company pays the basic wage and the parent company makes up the difference. This humane policy, however, is very costly and may well hamper the capacity of Japanese corporations to adjust quickly to changes in global markets. Recently, for example, Mitsubishi Heavy Industries, which has sent out 10,000 workers to other firms, is paying about $161 million a year to make up for their lost wages. According to the Sanwa Bank, Japanese companies are paying $26 billion in extra costs for an estimated 900,000 surplus workers. Other companies, however, are not doing as well. Recently Nippon Steel announced that it would institute a rotational system of layoffs where workers would be idled up to five or six days a month. However, they would still receive 70 percent of their pay for those days.[15]

There are other ways in which some companies, especially those in the secondary sector, are attempting to keep as many workers on as possible. Some companies are reducing prerequisites, such as free transportation and low cost housing. A few companies are considering hiring out workers to other companies that need temporary help. Older workers will face increasing pressure to retire early. For example, recently the president of Nippon Steel, Kiyoshi Yoneta, said that steel workers approaching retirement age could be asked to retire early and to go on unemployment in order to preserve the jobs of younger workers. Union leaders, on the other hand, are urging that the companies should adopt shorter working hours and work sharing alternatives. Other companies may be forced to abandon automatic wage raises based on seniority and impose wage freezes. None of these moves are popular with management, as well as labor, but both sides realize that with the rapid decline of the secondary sector, they have no alternative.[16]   At least to date there is little indication that Japanese companies will ask workers for wage reductions as have many American corporations, but it is possible that this could happen some day soon if conditions in this sector get any worse.

Japanese exporters have also been hurt badly by the rise of the yen against the dollar. The dramatic rise of the yen has hampered the ability of secondary sector companies to compete in export markets. Protectionist sentiment is growing in the United States and Europe, and foreign rivals are fighting back like never before. Far East competitors, such as Taiwan and South Korea, are exploiting their lower costs while U.S. and European companies are achieving efficiency gains and improvement in quality.

The high yen -- endaka in Japanese -- is slamming the nation's exporters two ways. Foreign competitors with costs dominated in dollars or French francs have more room to undercut Japanese companies on prices, and a dollar's worth of sales is worth less in yen.   The yen's steep appreciation has caused a drop in export volume and worsened export profitability, hurting manufacturing industries seriously. The household and non-manufacturing industries, by contrast, in 1987 were on a steady expansionary climb as a result of the price stabilization brought about by the strong yen and sagging crude oil prices. However, these industries' combined performance is lacking the strength needed to offset the slump in manufacturing. Thus, production activity remains stagnant and plant and equipment investment is decelerating.[17]

Tertiary Sector:

The big winner in the changing conditions of the Japanese economy is the service, or tertiary, sector. Here lies the future of Japan. It is those people engaged in such service industries as wholesale and retail trade, education, finance, insurance, real estate, transportation and communication, public utilities, public administration, and leisure activities who will prosper in the future.   The tertiary sector has played a major role in the modernization of Japan's economy and has always employed more workers than any other part of the economy. The tertiary sector grew very rapidly after the Meiji Restoration, especially in the fields of commerce, catering, and finance. There were less dramatic, but imporant gains in the transportation-communications and professional-public service areas throughout the Meiji Period.

All job categories in the tertiary sector have grown since 1955 with the greatest growth among clerical workers and sales personnel. The professional, managerial, and public administration categories have grown to a lesser extent, and there has been very little growth in such fields as domestic services and catering. Tertiary sector employment reached about 52 percent of the work force in 1985 and will continue to grow slowly in the late 1980s. If Japan becomes more of a welfare state, there will be a growth in the government sector. A genuinely growing area has been the leisure industry which has helped a simultaneous growth in certain facets of the advertising and transportation industries.

The rise of the leisure industry is due largely to rising wages, declining work hours, and the implementation of a five-day work week for many workers, along with physically less demanding work and changing social values. Virtually every Japanese home has a television set and there has been a vast increase in the number of pachinko (pinball) halls, racing tracks, bowling alleys, baseball stadiums, dance halls, cabarets, golf courses, and ski resorts. There has been a simultaneous boom in the hotel and travel industry as more Japanese take more frequent and longer vacations at home and abroad.

Japan is becoming one of the major banking centers of the world, and several Japanese banks rank among the biggest in the world. In 1986 Japan's largest bank, Dai-Ichi Kangyo, topped the list of the world's 100 largest banks, excluding those in the United States. Following Dai-Ichi Kangyo, the next four banks on the list were also Japanese: Fuji, Sumitomo, Mitsubishi and Sanwa. There were a total of thirty Japanese banks on the list.[18]

One of the most profitable ventures of these banks is foreign investment, mainly in the United States. According to *Business Week:*

America is running on Japanese money. Bulging with cash from their nation's exports, Japan's banks and security houses are moving funds into every nook of the U.S. While much of Japan's capital still seeks safe U.S. Treasury bonds, Japan's bankers are also reaching out into the heartland. By lending to Middle America, the Japanese are supporting the expansion of their manufacturers with money and information. "Japanese banks are moving hand-in-hand with Japanese companies as they expand in the U.S.," says Paul D. Mastroddi, a Morgan Guaranty Trust Co. specialist on Japanese banks.[19]

These Japanese banks owned $200 billion in US assets and had a net purchase of American government and corporate bonds of $65 billion in 1986. Fifty-five billion dollars of these purchases were government bonds, which means that the Japanese are playing a very important role in helping the American government finance its massive budget deficits.

Japan's future, however, is not limited to just banking and finance. There is a national effort involving both government and business to increase Japan's influence and growth in the area of high technology as well. One important policy concerns the effect of automation on the labor market. Auto producers like Toyota and Nissan are relying increasingly on the use of robotics in their factories. Among other plans for Japan's future are its much touted Fifth Generation computer project, an infant but active space program, and the designation of new towns as research centers and production hubs for new technologies.

Information and information-gathering are also becoming increasingly important for the Japanese economy. No other nation gathers information as assiduously as the Japanese. Every government, corporate, or trading office abroad, for example, has staffers who read the local press on a regular basis. Japanese know regional markets very well and use this knowledge to their advantage. Thus, a trading company with branches in New York and Beijing could provide an American company with much advice about establishing contacts in China. The selling and use of information will be even more beneficial to the Japanese in the future.

What effect will the current restructuring have on the Japanese economy? Government reports estimate that by the year 2000 restructuring in the Japanese economy will lead to an overall loss of a half million manufacturing jobs, but it is expected that growth in the tertiary sector will more than make up for this loss. In other words, Japan today is experiencing considerable disruption of its economy and many workers face future hardship, but this current spate of problems is probably temporary. MITI, for example, predicts that Japan will create 1.17 million new high technology and service jobs by the year 2000. The nation's rapidly growing financial sector is likely to lead the way as Japan becomes one of the leading financial centers in the world. Japanese bankers are becoming important investors, lenders, and providers of information. MITI believes that other growth industries in the tertiary sector will include leisure resorts and health spas are booming -- as well as telecommunications, information services, equipment leasing, temporary office services, and health care. Over the past few years, younger consumers have kept domestic consumption growing at a 3 percent rate.

Japan is also moving very successfully in the area of high tech. For example, the United States was once the leader in the production of semiconductors and other advanced and highly competitive high-tech goods. In the 1980s, however, the Japanese have caught up with their American competitors in many areas. Not long ago the United States enjoyed a nearly two-to-one lead in world market share of semi-conductors, but today Japan has a small, but rapidly growing, lead. Thus, the overall prognosis for the Japanese economy is very good.

CHAPTER IV- NOTES

1.   *Asahi Shimbun* (18 March 1987), p. 1.

2.   *Japan Times* (13 September 1986), p. 2.

3.   *The Wall Street Journal* (6 November 1986), p. 1.

4.   *Japan Times* (20 September 1986), p. 5.

5.   *Japan Economic Survey* (August 1987) p. 12.

6.   *Ibid.*

7.   *Ibid.*

8.   *Ibid.*

9.   Joel Dreyfus, "Fear and Trembling in the Colossus, *Fortune International* (30 March 1987), p. 32.

10.   *Japan Times Weekly* (11 April 1987), p. 5.

11.   Drefus, p. 34.

12.   *Japan Times Weekly* (11 April 1987), p. 4.

13.   *Dreyfus*, p. 34.

14.   Susan Chira, "A Job Crunch Jolts Japan," *The New York Times* (18 January 18 1987), sec. 3, p. 1.

15.   *Ibid.*, p. 18.

16.   *Ibid.*

17.   *Mitsubishi Bank Review* (January 1987), p. 1003.

18.   *Japan Times*, (2 August 1986), p. 5.

19.   "Japanese Capital Finds a Home in Middle America, *Business Week* (14 July 1986), p. 38-40.

CHAPTER V

GOVERNMENT AND BUSINESS

When foreigners talk about the relationship between government and business in Japan, one often gets the impression that there exists a steadfast partnership between the two. One hears of a Japanese government that is so actively pro-big business that it directs business "through a set of controls more refined than Karl Marx, V.I. Lenin, or Josef Stalin ever dreamed of."[1] Philip Trezise and Suzuki Yukio stress that in addition to normal monetary or fiscal policies, there are a

> "wide range of government measures, including direct controls and subsidies as well as other means of direction and persuasion" which have been "consciously and skillfully used to allocate the natural resources to those economic and industrial sectors that would provide the greatest returns in terms of growth. In effect, Japan has been looked on as an instance where planning and control in a considerable degree of detail have been tried and have worked, in some respects spectacularly well."[2]

Such statements have led more than a few foreigners to call the relationship between government and business "Japan, Inc." as if there were a monolithic organization there set to take charge of the world economy. To say that a "Japan Incorporated" exists would be ridiculous, but by the same token, it would be equally wrong to say that no relationship exists at all. Professor Edwin O. Reischauer summarizes government-business relations:

> The relationship in Japan between government and business is not that of mutually suspicious adversaries, as in the United States, but of collaborators. The contrast is so great that Americans have frequently exaggerated it, mistakenly claiming that government and business form a single entity -- "Japan, Inc." -- in which the government is said to control business completely or conversely a mysteriously unified big business world is said to control the government.[3]

Although it is definitely not "Japan, Inc.", the Japanese government has helped to promote big business whenever possible. When the Japanese began to industrialize during the latter part of the nineteenth century, the modern sectors of the economy received their first boost from the national government, which built mines, shipyards, and mills at its own expense and which then sold most of them to private firms at very cheap prices. Even after the government had divested itself of the factories it had built, it continued to shape and aid Japanese industry by granting subsidies and special privileges. Close ties existed between big business and the government before the Pacific War with the United States, but during the American Occupation of Japan (1945-52), such American concepts as free competition and adversary relationships between business and government were introduced. The dire political and economic conditions of the Occupation period, however, necessitated some form of delicate cooperation between businessmen and bureaucrats. During the postwar period, this cooperation has steadily increased.

Government-business relations are conducted in many ways and through many channels, the most important of which are the Ministry of International Trade and Industry (MITI) and the Ministry of Finance (MOF). While the Economic Planning Agency (EPA) is in charge of formulating broad economic objectives and forecasts, MITI sets goals for various industries and directs much of Japan's economic growth. It carefully supervised the acquisition of foreign technology by licensing foreign technology, establishing foreign exchange controls, and arranging that the finest technology is purchased under the most advantageous terms by those people or companies who are best equipped to use it.

The Japanese tax system is also geared to encourage rapid industrial growth, especially in certain key fields. The nation's central bank, the Bank of Japan, uses its immense power and influence to shape lending policies that favor growth industries and work against those that are in decline. These and other techniques allow a great deal of mutual coordination between business and government. Government cooperation was vital in the rebuilding of the steel, shipbuilding, coal, electrical power and fertilizer industries in the 1950s and 1960s and in the later development of the petrochemical, electronics, automobile, and chemical industries. In the 1980s the economic ministries have worked hard to encourage the development of "knowledge intensive" industries while gradually phasing out such labor intensive industries as textiles. The government encourages this transition by giving tax incentives to companies willing to make the shift to knowledge-intensive fields and by providing workers with retraining programs.

This mutual coordination between government and business, however, is not as monolithic or as dynamic as one might think. Japan has a powerful and expansive free enterprise economy and most decisions concerning business are made directly by the businesses themselves without any outside interference. Japanese businessmen almost universally give vigorous support to the free enterprise system and actively oppose any government attempts to regulate business too firmly. For example, innovative companies such as Sony forge ahead with little or no contact with the government. Occasional government assistance is useful, but too much government interference is something to be avoided.

As Ezra Vogel stressed in his book, *Japan as Number One*, a crucial function of government is information gathering. Unlike the United States where government and business often act as antagonists, in Japan there is a stress on close cooperation between the two camps. The Japanese government, with its many missions abroad and offices throughout Japan, gathers a wealth of information that is useful for business. This includes information on prices for raw materials around the world, facts concerning changing market conditions abroad, and moves by foreign governments that could affect Japanese interests. This information is shared with relevant businesses and industries to help them formulate their plans. Many Japanese corporations reciprocate; trading companies with branches abroad gather information which they share with government offices and other corporations. This sharing of information is yet another important bond between government and business in Japan.

It is also wrong to assume that business is the sole or even main concern of government. Japan has a vibrant parliamentary democracy, and the incumbent Liberal Democratic Party (LDP) must work to satisfy many diverse groups of which business is only one. For example, much of the party's support comes from residents of rural areas, many of whom are farmers, and this support is crucial to the future health of the LDP. Thus, the LDP must work very closely with agricultural interests. There are even times when some groups in the party support policies that conflict with those of other groups. For example, support for farmers wanting import quotas on certain agricultural goods might work against party support for further liberalization of trade relations with the United States.

It is important to understand that Japan's huge bureaucracy is not a monolithic organization working on behalf of business. Each ministry works hard to protect the interests of the sector it represents. Thus, the Ministry of Agriculture will lobby on behalf of farmers, fishermen, and those involved in forestry, and there are close ties between the ship building industry and the Ministry of Transport. Sometimes it is difficult to pool or coordinate the work of several diverse industries.

The Confucian Heritage:

Most books that deal with the relationship between business and government in Japan make little or no mention of the influence of Confucianism in Japan's political heritage. Confucianism is a hierarchical and practical socio-political philosophy that is designed to bring harmony and order to society. Confucians start out with the premise that while mankind is essentially good, people are corrupted because of ignorance. They do not know the true order of things; they fail to respect authority, to be responsible for those under their care, and to live in an appropriate manner.

Confucius believed that while benevolence (*jen*), justice (*i*), ceremony (*li*), knowledge (*chih*), and faith (*hsin*) are the most important virtues, benevolence (*jen*) is the virtue which must be at the heart of humanity. Confucius believed that man's fundamental goodness, as well as the natural affection existing between relatives within one family, is the cornerstone of social morality. Morality does not result from the commands of a deity; instead, it exists only when the bonds of genuine love found within the family are extended to all people. Then one can say that human nature has reached perfection and social order is being maintained in an appropriate manner. Those people who have attained this kind of perfect love of humanity are spoken of as men of benevolence, or virtue.[4]

Confucius believed that to become a virtuous and benevolent person must be the chief objective of all moral cultivation. Filial piety (*hsiao*) and the discharging of one's duty as a younger brother (*t'i*) have become very important virtues under Confucianism. Filial piety consists of respecting one's parents, taking care of them, and acting according to their wishes. Harmony is also important for the attainment of benevolence; harmony means that people in society have to be united in one accord and preserve this accord throughout society. Loyalty (*chung*) and faith (*hsin*) are the two virtues of sincerity. A sincere person does good not because he knows that it might get him some reward, but because he feels a genuine desire to do good unto others. Faith means serving others with utmost devotion. Confucius said that there are attributes that the "perfect gentleman" must adopt:

> They are a desire to see clearly when he looks at something; a desire to hear every detail when listening to something; a desire to present a tranquil countenance; a desire to preserve an attitude of respect; a desire to be sincere in his words; a desire to be careful in his work; a willingness to enquire further into anything about which he has doubts; a willingness to bear in mind the difficulties consequent on anger; a willingness to consider moral values when presented with the possibility of profit.[5]

Confucius was very concerned about the relationship between king and citizen and the role of government in society. Confucius advocated the concept of virtuous government, which strengthens the people by means of morality and serves to bring about order in society by raising the level of virtue among the people. Thus, the function of government is to act as a role model. If the leaders act in a correct manner and guide the people with love, honor, dignity, and decorum, the people will behave likewise. If the government becomes corrupt and sets a bad example for the people to follow, then the people too will become bad. What is important here is that the government is supposed to set the tone for society and that the citizenry must engage in a pattern of life designed by the state.

Japan is often correctly defined as a Confucian country, but there are some very sharp differences between Japanese and Chinese Confucianism. Historically, a critical departure in Japan is the lesser role of the idea of benevolence, which became the central virtue of Chinese Confucianism. In Japan, loyalty developed into the most important virtue; the Japanese are supposed to follow the government's dictates without asking any provocative questions.

There is, however, even a difference in the way the two cultures look at the idea of loyalty. In China, loyalty means that one has to be true to one's conscience, but in Japan, it means total devotion to one's lord to the point of sacrificing oneself:[6]

> Consequently, Confucius' words 'act with loyalty in the service of one's lord' were interpreted by the Chinese to mean 'Retainers must serve their lord with a sincerity which does not conflict with their own consciences,' whereas the Japanese interpreted the same words as 'Retainers must devote their whole lives to their lord.' As a result, loyalty in Japan was a concept which, in conjunction with filial piety and duty to one's seniors, formed a trinity of values which regulated within society the hierarchic relationships based on authority, blood ties and age respectively.[7]

The Japanese have had a more one-sided view of government and government authority than the Chinese since the medieval period. In China, government officials were chosen through competitive examinations, meaning that there was no permanent ruling class. The citizenry theoretically had the right to overthrow any government that does not look after the welfare of society. In Japan of the Tokugawa era (1600-1867), on the other hand, there was a permanent ruling class, there were no open exams for government posts, and the citizenry was not accorded the right of revolt under any circumstances. Merchants were at the bottom of the social scale and had few rights despite their comparative wealth. There is thus a tradition in Japan that one owes obedience, loyalty and respect to the government. Leadership--both good and bad--stems from the government, and business must look up to the government for leadership and guidance. Today, although there is much less subservience to the government on the part of business, many Japanese businessmen expect close ties between government and business. Thus, a close partnership between government and business seems quite natural for the Japanese.

The Japanese view of the state is rooted in familialism:

> In the traditional view, the whole nation is a family; what the house is to a biological family, the state is to the

> national family. The state is not merely a part of the system, but the very framework of it. The Japanese feel that in the beginning there was the nation house called Japan and the people were born into it.... The state bureaucrats exercise authority not in the name of the people, but in the name of the House of Japan. To the Japanese way of thinking, then, the state does not "interfere" with the affairs of private business. It merely manages itself, exercising authority and control of its constituencies. The productive activities of private businesses is very much a part of the business of the whole nation-state.[8]

Thus, the Japanese see their nation as an extended family. There is a national consensus that Japan must be a world economic power and that it is the duty of all Japanese to sacrifice themselves for this national goal.

Japan's Industrial Policy - The Economic Background:

The concept "Industrial Policy" (IP) is frequently used to describe the planning required for optimum growth in the Japanese economy. The objective of IP is to help raise the real income of the population by shifting resources to specific industries in which they can be most productive, thereby gaining international competitive advantage for Japan. It is a set of "policies and methods used primarily to increase the productivity of factor inputs and to influence, directly or indirectly, the investment (and disinvestment) decisions of industries."[9]

In Japan these policies and methods typically relate to areas such as trade, labor markets, competition policy, and tax incentives. The means to carry out the policy goals includes the following: a broad range of trade protection measures, subsidies in various forms, de jure and de facto exemptions from anti-trust statutes, several types of labor market adjustments, and a variety of mostly direct and often industry-specific assistance to enhance the pace and range of adoption of new technology. Rather than producing a very broad range of goods, the Japanese have selected a few areas where they can produce a vast quantity of certain goods at competitive prices in a quality manner.[10] A good example is cameras. Thirty years ago the Germans made many of the best cameras in the world, but today the Japanese dominate the camera industry.

Historically, there have been three main elements in Japanese industrial development:[11]

1)   The need for the development of a highly competitive manufacturing sector;

2)   The deliberate restructuring of industry overtime toward higher value-added, higher productivity industries -- today these are mainly knowledge-intensive tertiary sector industries; and

3)   Aggressive domestic and international business strategies.

Japan has few natural resources and is dependent on massive imports of raw materials.   Japan must export to pay for the imports and manufacturing and the sales of its services (such as banking and finance) are the only means of paying for the imports. Thus, the careful development and guidance of the producing sector has been a key concern of both the government and the people of Japan since the start of the Meiji era. Since World War II the Japanese government has devised an Industrial Policy that has the general goal of bringing an overall "strengthening of international competitiveness" of various modern industries to Japan.

> To enable a nation dependent for its basic resources on foreign countries to catch up in a relatively short time with the advanced   nations, it was necessary to rapidly expand imports of raw materials, which would be accompanied by the rapid growth of the domestic economy. Rapid growth in the exports of various industrial products was, therefore, the most essential condition for maintaining the international trade balance under the circumstances.[12]

Japanese government and business leaders both agree that the composition of the country's output must continually shift if living standards are to rise.[13] Thus, while in the 1950s Japan's exports were mainly unskilled and labor-intensive (eg., toys and textiles), by the 1960s Japan's exports were more capital-intensive (eg., steel and ships). In the 1970s more complex products, such as cars and color television sets, gained prominence, while in the 1980s Japan has been moving into high technology and sophisticated service industries. The Japanese government has played an active role in making these shifts, often acting in anticipation of certain economic developments rather than reacting to them. For example, in the late 1970s the Japanese government saw the need for a shift to knowledge-intensive industries. Government support for research and development grew rapidly, and large joint government-industry development projects in computers and machine tools were started. At the same time, the government saw the need to help manage the decline of such competitively troubled industries as textiles, shipbuilding, and chemical fertilizers.

The essential ingredient in industrial policy, however, is not the government's role but, rather, that of individual firms:

> Industrial policies simply forced "from above" are not necessarily long-lived. To keep these policies in long-term effect, there must be aggressive response in the private industries "from below." In Japan's case, too, the success of guidance from above was only made possible by dynamism in industrial circles.[14]

As noted in Chapter Two, it is the Japanese *kaisha* that have brought economic success to Japan rather than the government. Japan's export successes are the result of aggressive business strategies, access to information, and solid management. When planning for the long-term, Japanese *kaisha* try to achieve the lowest possible cost in producing and distributing a product.

Industrial Policy and Implementation:

While business leaders in the West often view government initiatives towards industrial policy with suspicion and hostility, Japanese traditionally have allowed for a legitimate government role in both shaping and carrying out industrial policy. Senior businessmen often view government guidance of industry as something quite normal and equate the success of their firms with the greater good of Japan. The Diet (parliament) passes legislation which only enunciates essential policy; it is up to the ministries, which are staffed by a large and highly competent core of career officials, to develop coherent programs, draft legislation, and carry out this legislation.[15] The historical roots of modern industrial policy date back to the Meiji Restoration:

> In 1868 Japan was abruptly opened to world trade after centuries of economic isolation. The density of the population and the mountainous landscape ruled out large-scale

agriculture and dictated industrialization as the path to higher income and trade. The government's response to this challenge set the tone for Japanese industrial policy to follow. Japan's new leaders recruited an elite, central bureaucracy from the able samurai whose interests were nationalist and whose perspective was modern. Isolated from the Western debate on political economy (socialism versus capitalism), they were pragmatic rather than ideological in their thinking. They did not fear concentration of industrial or financial power, and in fact encouraged such concentration as a point of contact and coordination with the central ministries. Rapid capital accumulation had to be encouraged. After some limited early experiments in state entrepreneurship, the government played only a small direct or regulatory role in the 19th century's rapid industrialization of Japan, but the state, as an architect, catalyst, and coordinator of industrial policy, dominated the policymaking process.[16]

The Economic Ministries:

The two leading government ministries that work with the business sector are the Ministry of Finance (MOF) and the Ministry of International Trade and Industry (MITI). They provide extensive leadership, direction, and advice for the business community and are the architects of industrial policy.

The Ministry of Finance

The MOF carries operational responsibilities forall of Japan's fiscal affairs, including the preparation of the national budget. It also plays the primary role in international monetary and domestic financial affairs. It initiates fiscal policies and, through its control over the Bank of Japan, is responsible for monetary policy as well. MOF also allocates public investment, formulates tax policies and collects taxes, and regulates foreign commerce and exchange.

Monetary policy pertains to the regulation, availability, and cost of credit, while fiscal policy deals with government expenditures, taxes, and debt. Through these measures MOF regulates the allocation of resources in the economy, affects the distribution of income and wealth among the citizenry, stabilizes the level of economic activities, and promotes economic growth and welfare.

The MOF has played a very important role in Japan's post-war economic growth. It has advocated a "growth-first" approach that is based on a high proportion of government spending going into capital accumulation and minimal government spending, which keeps both taxes and deficit financing down, thus making more money available for private investment. Most Japanese have traditionally put money into accounts at savings banks. Due to artificially low interest rates, industries can afford to borrow a great deal of capital, which promotes industrial expansion.

There is no other ministry or government office with as much prestige as the MOF. Every year it accepts only about 20 to 25 new permanent employees, many of whom are graduates of the Faculty of Law at Tokyo University. Many retired members of the Ministry have had very successful careers in politics or public life. There is often some public resentment over the elite nature of the Ministry and its workers, but workers are also generally respected for their competence, dedication, and hard work. Some Japanese journalists have gone as far as to call them the "samurai of the Japanese government."

Ministry of International Trade and Industry

While the MOF controls the monetary and financial aspects of the economy, MITI is responsible for the regulation of production and distribution of goods and services. It is the "steward" of the Japanese economy and provides business with a sense of direction. It does a great deal of planning concerning the structure of Japanese industry.

MITI has six special functions. First, it is responsible for the control of Japan's foreign trade and the supervision of international commerce. Second, it is charged with the responsibility of assuring the smooth flow of goods in the national economy. Third, it has jurisdiction over the manufacturing, mining, and distribution industries and is in charge of promoting their development. Fourth, it secures for Japan a reliable supply of raw materials and energy resources. Fifth, it administers the government's policies towards small businesses. Sixth, it promotes and guides the growth of small business. The first three are the main functions of the MITI; it controls international trade, regulates the production and distribution of goods, and makes every effort to shape Japanese industry to meet the challenges of the future:

> In sectors of policy interest, MITI collects a good deal of market and competitive data, gives administrative guidance to firms, and issues a lot of paper in support of a policy. Communication between MITI and individual producers takes place frequently at several levels. Some observers of this process have mistakenly concluded that MITI is dictating investment rates in the industry. This is not MITI's intention. Market prospects, not ministries, stimulate investment in growth businesses and ultimately discourage investment in declining ones. MITI understands that it would be counterproductive to force wary producers to invest. Nor can a ministry know any particular business sector well enough to design or direct a specific series of investments. Instead, MITI tries to develop a shared perception of a business' future and designs incentives and subsidies to accelerate the desired course.[17]

Administrative guidance (*gyosei shido*) is MITI's main instrument of enforcement. It is a method used extensively by the Japanese government to support or to enhance a wide range of policies. It involves the use of influence, prestige, advice, and persuasion to encourage both corporations and individuals to work in particular directions that the government sees as desirable. The persuasion is exerted and the advice is given by public officials who often have the power to either provide or withhold the following: loans, grants, subsidies, licenses, tax concessions, government contracts, permissions to import, foreign exchange, and approval of cartel arrangements. Thus, the Japanese have developed administrative guidance as a means to buffer market swings, to anticipate market developments, and to enhance market competition.

It is inaccurate to think of administrative guidance just in terms of "carrot and stick." Rather, the Japanese tradition of private acceptance of government leadership, the traditional Confucian view that one must respect the ability of the government to work on behalf of the nation, and the realization that bureaucrats in the top government ministries have knowledge, experience, and information superior to that available to the ordinary firm make administrative guidance far more effective than it would be in the United States.[18] No firm is fully obliged to accept government guidance. Some firms in such rapidly expanding areas as high tech have formulated their own plans, often without the "advice and consent" of the government.

MITI, however, is not alone in formulating industrial policies. The Ministry of Agriculture initiates policies for agriculture and for the food processing industry, the Ministry of Transport is responsible for shipping and other transportation industries, and the Ministry of Finance watches overbanking, insurance, and securities concerns.

The Ministry of Transport's planned shipbuilding program for Japan's merchant marine is an example of industrial policy at work. The program, first begun in 1947, involves yearly consultations between the ministry and representatives of the Shipping and Ship Building Rationalization Council. Together they decide on the tonnage and types of ships to be built and the allocation of production contracts among the applicant firms. Ship building firms that receive the contracts receive preferential financing from banks and are in turn subject to close governmental supervision.

The three broad industrial policy concerns of MITI and the other industrial ministries are: investment rate and structure of producers, technology development, and export-import measures.[19]

Investment Rate and Structure of Producers:

The Japanese government has historically adopted various policies generally favorable to capital investment, including no capital gains taxes on securities, central bank permanent control of interest rates, a strong anti-inflation commitment, and few administrative barriers. MITI, however, often does not stand in favor of investment by all competitors in any given area. When a certain industry is growing rapidly, MITI prods an industry to consolidate; for example, several companies are merged into one.[20] In declining or stagnant industries, MITI urges capacity retirement. The aim of MITI is to accelerate market forces and to bring about more stable competition among a few relatively low cost producers. Nurturing new industries has also been an important goal:

> MITI used administrative guidance, import restriction, coordination of investment in plant and equipment, merger

and other methods of production consolidation, approval of cartels, postponing of liberalization of direct investment from outside, tax incentives for leading industries, low interest loans, and other measures. Because of these measures, the steel and automobile industries, for example, have now acquired a leading world position, although their international competitiveness had not been high at the time when their products' prices in the world market were relatively expensive.[21]

Technology Development:

This concern has grown as Japan has moved toward more knowledge-intensive industries. The government finances only a few projects and uses a variety of incentives for private development. In many cases the government uses tax credits, grants, loans, and association sponsorship to encourage corporate research and development.

Export-Import Measures:

The third major concern of Japanese industrial policy has been international trade. In the early 1970s the Japanese government stimulated exports, restricted manufactured imports, and assisted large-scale material imports, but these policies have changed radically in the 1980s. Today broad export incentives are gone, and restrictions on imports have been eliminated.

It should be noted, however, that one of the basic factors which made export promotion easier in Japan was the huge domestic market of approximately 100 million people. The large-scale production of certain goods to meet domestic needs could easily be expanded for export purposes at prices lower than other countries could manufacture the same goods:

> If the domestic market expands in line with or ahead of export expansion, a product with a relatively higher rate of expansion would be subject to a considerable reduction in unit cost through mass production, thus allowing an increase in exports. In other words, even though the relationship between the expansion of the domestic and export markets might have been that of a trade-off on an extremely short-term basis, it proved to be highly complementary for the mid- and long-term. The existence of a feedback relationship between expansion of domestic demand and exports resulted in high growth in Japan.[22]

Industrial Reorganization:

Industrial reorganization is a major concern of MITI. MITI traditionally has been concerned with the excessive fragmentation and resulting weakness of various key industries. The liberalization of foreign investment, which was completed by the early 1970s, was thought to have exposed small firms in a number of crucial industries to foreign takeover. MITI's response was to achieve greater concentration of production in fewer and larger firms. Thus, when liberalization of trade began in the 1960s, MITI began sponsoring company mergers.

MITI's industrial reorganization efforts have had mixed results. Mergers, especially large mergers, are difficult to arrange. Businessmen are often reluctant to approve of government intervention in their businesses and are afraid that the merger of two firms will adversely affect the intricate employee structural relationships and loyalties within each firm. The Fair Trade Commission, the purpose of which is to halt the over-concentration of Japanese industry, has at times successfully halted MITI mergers. Thus, while MITI has succeeded in working out several important mergers, there have been some failures as well.

Private Institutions:

There are also some important private institutions that also influence industrial policy. The four major business management associations are led by Keidanren (Federation of Economic Organization) whose membership includes the leadership of 700 large corporations. These organizations speak on behalf of business and their leaders meet on a frequent basis with government and political leaders. They also provide the governing Liberal Democratic Party with substantial funding. Private industry associations are concerned with government policy toward individual sectors and try to maintain a working relationship with MITI's industrial bureaus and lobbying groups. The thirteen large commercial banks ("city banks"), which extend about a quarter of the loans made by financial institutions in Japan, are interested in industrial policy because some of their heaviest borrowers are Japan's leading industrial firms.[23]

Conclusion:

The Japanese government is one-tenth the size of the American government, but efficiently manages a population almost exactly half that of the United States. Japan's Confucian tradition has helped to instill a feeling of loyalty and respect for the government by the Japanese people. There is the popular notion that government is there to work on behalf of the people and that government leaders, who, today, are among the best educated and most dedicated workers in Japan, have strong leadership qualities. Japanese are not as suspicious of big government as are most Americans and many Japanese businessmen do not see the government as an adversary but, rather, as a partner with a common purpose -- economic prosperity for Japan.

CHAPTER V - NOTES

1.   Richard Halloran, *Japan: Images and Realities* (New York: Random House, 1969), p. 133.

2.   Philip H. Trezise and Suzuki Yukio, "Politics, Government and Economic Growth in Japan," in Hugh Patrick and Henry Rosovsky, Eds., *Asia New Giant: How theJapanese Economy Works* (Washington, DC: Brookings Institution, 1976), p. 755.

3.   Edwin Reischauer, *The Japanese* .(Cambridge, MA: Harvard University Press, 1977), p. 191.

4.   Michio Morishima, *Why Has Japan Succeeded? Western Technology and the Japanese Ethos* (Cambridge: Cambridge University Press, 1982), p. 3.

5.   *The Analects of Confucius*, Chapter 16, quoted in Morishima, pp. c Patterns in the Japanese Economy (Tokyo: Tokyo University Press, 1982), p. 21.

13.   *Ibid.*, p. 7.

14.   *Shinohara*, p. 23.

15.   *Ibid.*, p. 36.

16.   *Ibid.*, pp. 36-37.

17.   *Ibid.*, p. 46.

18.   *Ibid.*

19.   *Ibid.*, p. 48.

20.   The 1970 MITI recommendation that Fuji Steel and Yawata Steel merge is a case in point. After the merger, the new company, Nippon Steel, was to control 36% of the industry's production volume. The result was an amazing jump in the production, efficiency, and research capacity of the new company. See Shinohara, p. 46.

21.   Shinohara, p. 48.

22.   *Ibid.*, p. 23.

23.   *Ibid.*, p. 45-46.

U.S.-JAPANESE ECONOMIC RELATIONS IN THE 1980s

Since 1985 Japan has evolved into a major financial power that is using its new wealth to carve out a position of strength among many fronts of the American economy. Japan is rapidly becoming one of the world's major financial centers. Japanese corporations are investing billions of dollars of their surplus cash in bonds, stocks, real estate, and manufacturing in the United States each year. The success of the Japanese has bred jealously between the two nations, as well as a sense of strident nationalism among many Japanese who now refuse to view Japan as an economic dwarf accepting orders from the American giants. The result has been a decline in the once strong friendship between Japan andthe United States, and the well-being of both states is endangered.

American-Japanese relations reached a new low in the spring of 1987 when the Reagan Administration enacted its 100 percent tariffs on selected Japanese imports, like computer chips, and the House of Representatives passed a strongly protectionist tradebill. Certain American political leaders are under the illusion that the United States can take harsh measures against the Japanese with impunity. Recent reports indicate that many Japanese political and business leaders are getting tired of anti-Japanese noise in Washington. They know that Japan is fully capable of a form of retaliation that would have an immediate and rather devastating effect on the American economy, although such a retaliation would be damaging to the Japanese as well.

In recent years Japanese investors have been very active at the quarterly auctions of the Federal Reserve when it conducts its auctions of Treasury Bonds. This quarterly ritual relies heavily on the Japanese investor to continue financing the deficit-ridden federal budget at relatively low interest rates. At the auction in February, 1987, Japanese investors bought upward of 40 percent of the 30-year bonds issued.[1] To put it simply, the Japanese are funding much of our growing debt: our current prosperity is being propelled by money from Tokyo. The Japanese are reinvesting much of the money that they make from the trade deficit back into the United States. What would happen if the Japanese suddenly decided to stop buying U.S. bonds?

Japanese financial analysts are urging Japanese businessmen to diversify out of bonds and into American, as well as Australian, Canadian, and European stockmarkets. Even a small "diminution of Japanese participation could drive the yields on Treasury bonds appreciably higher. The ripple effect would produce a costly burden on Americans across the board, from home-owners shopping for mortgages to businessmen contemplating new investments, and could, at worst, hurl the economy into an inflationary nightmare."[2] President Reagan was correct when he vetoed the 1987 protectionist trade bill and only imposed temporary largely symbolic tariffs on some Japanese goods. It is the United States that must fear Japanese retaliation and not the reverse. Anti-American feelings are growing in Japan, and suchfeelings will eventually take their toll on financial markets. It is sheer folly to think that the U.S. can impose penalties on Japan without paying a price somewhere down the line.

The Japanese have the power to retaliate against Washington by simply not cooperating. If they stopped buying bonds, cut back on Wall Street, or ceased investing elsewhere, the effect would be felt quickly. The present mood of Japan's Ministry of International Trade and Industry (MITI), however, is to placate Americans whenever possible. According to a Japanese reporter who covers MITI, "The Japanese government still respects the power and influence of the United States and realizes that Japanese prosperity depends on close relations with Washington. The mood at MITI is closer to compromise or even appeasement rather than outright defiance. Even if Reagan or other American officials seem unfair to the Japanese government, it seems best to let the American lions roar."[3]

To put it simply, neither Japan nor the United States can survive without the other. These two nations have enjoyed a close relationship that is akin to a stormy but intimate marriage. The United States was the first Western nation to "open" Japan in the 1850s and ties have remained close ever since. Americans have always dreamed of the illusive China market, but trade with Japan has always outstripped that of trade with China. War brought a temporary divorce in this old marriage, but it was the United States that defeated Japan and played the crucial role in rebuilding Japan after World War II during the Occupation. American military officers even wrote the current Japanese constitution in 1947 under the explicit orders of General MacArthur.

Economic problems in both countries have put a severe strain on relations between the two states. These problems can be divided into two general areas: product specific actions like dumping, import quotas and voluntary export quotas; and macro-incidents, like the foreign exchange value of the yen, the Japanese trade surplus, and Japanese policies concerning the inflow of foreign investment. The product-specific problems developed first in the late 1950s while macro-incidents occurred with increasing frequency in the late 1960s:

> In both types of incidents the U.S. government took the initiative and asked or demanded a change in policies affecting Japan's exports, its imports, its trade surplus, and the exchange rate. Most policy measures were adopted by the Japanese. The initial motivation for American demands was the complaint of American producers of import-competing goods. Then U.S. firms wanted easier access to the Japanese market, both as a market for U.S. produced goods and as a source of supply for U.S. goods. Finally, the U.S. government was concerned about the impact of Japanese macro-variables on U.S. macro-variables; a substantial part of the variations in the U.S. trade and payment balances was the mirror of the variations in the Japanese trade and payments balances.[4]

Product-Specific Incidents:

This area can be divided into several categories, the most troublesome of which covers Japanese exports to the United States. The tremendous surge of American imports from Japan, which began in the early 1960s and has continue unabated in the late 1980s, has resulted in a huge trade surplus in Japan's favor and losses for American producers of competitive goods. The major reason for the complaints by American producers is that most U.S. imports from Japan are highly competitive with American domestic production while only a tiny handful of American goods sent to Japan are competitive with Japanese products. Moreover, the Japanese demand for commodities in the 1970s was growing at a rate three times that of the

United States. This means that U.S. imports did not seriously hurt the sale of Japanese products in Japan, whereas Japanese imports occupied more of the U.S. market, thereby reducing the sale of American-made products in the U.S. In some product lines, U.S.imports of Japanese products grew so rapidly that several American firms had to abandon production.

Macro-incidents:

The Japanese have made concerted attempts to adjust the foreign exchange value of the yen, to reduce Japanese trade surplus, and to encourage the inflow of foreign investment into Japan. The yen has been allowed to find its own place on the international money market. There has also been a genuine liberalization of foreign trade in Japan. The few restricted products are agricultural. Thus, however grudgingly, the Japanese are making some attempts to accede to American demands.

The United States and Japan in the late 1980s:

During the 1980s there has been a growing economic interdependence between Japan and the United States. The importance of the United States as a market for Japanese manufacturers has continued to increase with the United States receiving 37.2 percent of Japan's exports in 1985 compared to only 24.2% in 1980. At the same time, Japan has remained the largest and most stable customer for American-made manufactured goods, as well as agricultural and industrial raw products, such as West Virginia coal. A visitor to the beautiful harbor at Hampton and Newport News, Virginia, for example, will witness a constant stream of ships full of coal bound for Japan. Japan continues to rank only behind Canada as a market for American goods as the Pacific Basin has replaced the Atlantic as the leading region for American trade.

The 1980s has also marked Japan's emergence as an important supplier of capital to the United States while Japan has continued to receive considerable investments from the United States. For example, Japan's net purchase of U.S. Treasury obligations jumped from an estimated $6.1 billion in 1984 to $19.2 billion the following year, while the net purchase of U.S. securities by Japanese investors nearly tripled to $29.9 billion in the same time frame. These trends continued in 1986 when Japanese investors invested nearly half of their $132 billion foreign investments in U.S. government and corporate bonds.[5]

The quickening pace of American-Japanese economic integration in the mid-1980s has created numerous problems, fears, and frictions on both sides of the Pacific. The most difficult problem is the rapidly growing trade deficit which expanded in Japan's favor from $19.3 billion in 1983 to $58.6 billion in 1986.[6] This growing expansion of red ink played a role in the rapid deterioration of the overall United States trade account in the mid-1980s (American exports to Japan totaled $26.9 billion in 1986 while the Japanese sent $85.5 billion worth of goods to the United States). This came at a time when the United States had just become the world's greatest debtor with a huge trade deficit of $169.8 billion in 1986.[7] This is in direct contrast to Japan, which in 1986 became the world's largest net creditor nation.[8]

Increased trade frictions between Japan and the United States and sanctions imposed by the United States on Japan in April of 1987 after the U.S. accused Japan of continuing to "dump" semiconductor chips have had a very negative impact on the way people of both nations perceive each other. In a poll conducted in May, 1987, by *The New York Times* in both Japan and the United States, it was found that after months of trade friction between the United States and Japan, a majority of Japanese polled consider relations between the two nations as being unfriendly.[9] This was in sharp contrast to the results of a 1986 poll, which showed only 30 percent of the Japanese polled characterizing relations this way. The Japanese are becoming increasingly irritated at the way both governments are handling the trade problem. They feel that Tokyo and Washington are not doing enough to correct the trade imbalance and are quite pessimistic over the prospect of trade relations in the next few years. The Japanese public, however, was overwhelmingly opposed to retaliation by Japan against the April, 1987 sanctions imposed on Japan by the United States.[10]

Another public opinion poll taken in Japan before the imposition of the Reagan tariffs in April, 1987, indicated that the number of Japanese feeling "close" to America had fallen to its lowest level in a decade -- a trend that surely has been exacerbated by the tariffs. In April, 1987, *Newsweek* surveyed the shelves of Japanese bookstores and found a proliferation of titles like *Traps Set by America*, *The Japan-U.S. War Has Not Ended*, and *Can America be Trusted?*[11]

Unlike the Japanese, only 19 percent of Americans polled by the *New York Times* called ties between Washington and Tokyo unfriendly. This figure, however, was a full 10 percentage points higher than in 1986 and 12 points higher than 1985. If these figures are truly representative, it is possible that members of the U.S. Congress are overreacting in their negative comments about Japan and in their efforts to impose trade barriers with Tokyo. Another possible interpretation of these figures is that Americans are not as aware of the trade crisis between Washington and Tokyo as are the Japanese. As a result, the American public is less antagonistic to the Japanese.

It is ironic that tensions are growing at a time of increased cooperation between the United States and Japan in a number of areas, including defense. During five years of negotiations between the Reagan and Nakasone administrations, both governments have reached an unprecedented degree of understanding concerning Japan's strategic role in the Pacific. Japan's 1987 military budget of $32 billion, while small by American or Soviet standards, now ranks third in the world. Japan has also begun the slow but important process of living up to its commitment to the United States to safeguard its own sea lanes up to 1,000 miles off the Japanese coast -- most importantly, the lanes heading south to the Philippines.[12]

American sales to Japan consist of roughly equal dollar amounts of food, raw materials, chemicals, manufactured goods, machinery, and lesser amounts of coal, oil, airplanes, and airplane parts. Roughly 80 percent of Japan's exports to the United States include nearly equal shares of cars, trucks, automobile parts, consumer electronic goods, and office and other machinery. Other manufactured goods and steel account for the rest of Japanese exports bought by Americans.[13]

Americans have been major sellers of raw materials and food products to the Japanese, but it is unlikely that the Japanese market for these goods will grow much in the future. The rapid decline of the Japanese steel industry and increased purchases of coal from China and the Soviet Union may hurt U.S. sales of coal to Japan. Canadian lumber sales to Japan have undercut the expected growth of sales from American timber companies in Washington and Oregon. Even American sales of agricultural commodities have grown less than expected. For example, other nations have succeeded in breaking the stranglehold the United States has had on Japan's feed corn market. Japanese trading companies are now buying significant amounts of corn from China and Argentina. In recent years Chinese corn has been priced below American corn and it has both a higher protein content and a lower moisture content. The Japanese bought large amounts of American soybean products in the mid-1980s, but American farmers were forced into increased competition from Brazilian producers of soy. Thus, while American producers of primary products still continue to do well in Japan, the lower prices and increased quality of goods from other nations have cut deeply into the United States' traditional market share in Japan.[14]

One must also not forget that while the price of manufactured goods imported from Japan continues to rise, such primary products as coal and food have not risen much in price over the past decade. This factor further contributes to the growing trade imbalance between the United States and Japan.

The Japanese have always purchased a significant amount of high quality capital goods from the United States. The expanding Japanese market for factory and office automation equipment has meant additional sales opportunities for American manufacturers of computer systems and peripheral equipment. Japanese purchases of commercial aircraft from such companies as Boeing also continue to grow. On the other hand, the Japanese have not purchased as many American consumer goods in the mid-1980s as had been hoped by the Reagan adminstration.[15]

Americans, on the other hand, have continued their evergrowing purchases of Japanese manufactured goods. The rise of the value of the yen has raised the dollar price of Japanese cars in the United States; therefore, increased competition from South Korea and Yugoslavia has diverted the attention of some Americans in search of inexpensive cars. Nonetheless, the demand for Japanese automobiles remains strong. Each year in the mid-

1980s, Americans have bought over 2.5 million Japanese cars as opposed to 8 to 8.5 million domestically produced cars. Smaller Japanese automobile producers of Isuzu, Suzuki, and Mitsubishi have been increasing their American market share, and Japanese automakers as a whole have continued their profitable move into the midsize and luxury markets that are Detroit's mainstay and into America's growing and highly competitive small truck market. The roughly 19.2 million Japanese vehicles sold in the United States between 1978 and 1985 has also meant an enormous market for Japanese replacement parts, and the large Japanese auto plants in the U.S. have relied greatly on Japanese producers of auto parts.[16]

The value of the dollar slid steadily between 1985 and 1987, precipitated by the finance ministers and central bankers of the G-5 nations who met in New Yorkin September, 1985, and who agreed to work on a concerted effort to push down the overvalued dollar. Over the next two years the yen rose by 100 yen, or 70% against the dollar -- from 240 to 140 yen.[17] The higher yen, however, failed to make a noticeable impact in reducing the surplus in Japan's trade balance. Thus, the surplus in Japan's trade balance totaled $101.4 billion in fiscal 1986, a dramatic increase over the $61.6 billion recorded in fiscal 1985, and the highest surplus recorded anywhere. Reasons for this surplus include the large decrease in the price of oil and a rapid increase in parts exported to serve Japanese factories abroad.[18]

Thus, at least in the immediate future, the prognosis is for a continuation of the same trends of the recent past and a probable expansion of the current trade deficit. The further lowering of Japanese trade barriers in the area of agriculture would only have a minimal effect on the trade balance. Further protectionist measures by Washington might only convince some Japanese to buy their agricultural goods elsewhere at lower prices. The American government must proceed with great caution in its dealings with the Japanese.

"The Real Cause" of the U.S. Trade Deficit - A Japanese Perspective:

Japan's emergence in the mid-1980s as a major financial power has spurred a growth of nationalism among some Japanese financial leaders and writers. They are no longer content to play "second fiddle" to the United

States and strongly resent the growing "Japan-bashing" so often found in the American press and in the U.S. Congress. Masahiko Ishizuka, a writer for Japan's leading financial newspaper, the *Nihon Keizai Shimbun* (*Japan Economic Journal*) presents a recent Japanese perspective on the growing U.S. trade deficit with Japan:

> With the Japanese currency continuing strong against the U.S. dollar, the export industries -- especially automobiles and consumer electronics -- are trying hard to survive by strengthening their operations domestically. 'Let's make ourselves strong enough to withstand this ordeal of a high yen,' appears to be the slogan across the nation. But at least one leading economist suggests that Japan's ability to adjust to the climb of the yen will mean an endless cycle of monetary trauma -- a revaluation treadmill.
>
> It is ironic that Japan's ability to withstand the strong yen is tied to the notion of sacrifice. One banker says, 'If we continue like this, we will be slave laborers to the world forever.' He feels that the yen is overvalued, exposing Japanese industry to hardship, and not solving Japanese trade problems.
>
> Some industrialists and commentators are beginning to voice their dissatisfaction with what they see as Prime Minister Yasuhiro Nakasone's overly conciliatory attitude toward Washington. Their criticisms are rooted in recognition of the troubled Japan-U.S. economic relationship. They argue that Japan should have asked the Americans to spend and borrow less and save more, instead of listening to American demands that the Japanese spend more and save less. The overvaluation of the yen, according to the critics, merely reflects an undervaluation of the dollar, for which the United States is responsible.
>
> Instead of asserting the Japanese position, Japanese politicians have capitulated to the U.S. demands that Japan accept responsibility for the trade imbalance because of its restrictions on imports and weak currency. 'What Nakasone did was make one unilateral concession after another to President Reagan, always yielding to the U.S. demand that Japan be the one to initiate changes,' charges one critic. The series of concessions that Japan has introduced under pressure from the U.S. has always been accompanied by extreme reluctance, but never self-assertion, according to the criticism. This is simply an extension of the attitude that has characterized Japanese relations with the U.S. since the close of the Pacific War.
>
> The real cause of the deficits in the U.S. economy is the unreasonable strength of domestic demand there -- especially personal consumption. No nation in the world has yet

succeeded in reducing its external deficits without holding down domestic demand, and the U.S. can hardly expect to be an exception. This means that Americans must accept a decline in their standard of living to relieve their nation's economic woes -- woes they mistakenly blame on the Japanese and others.

The country that has played the role of unchallenged leader of the postwar world, believing itself free to force others to change at its whim, must now remove itself from its catatonia, admit its mistakes, and seek the initiative to correct its problems.

This is an argument that Japanese officials have yet to voice in economic debates with their U.S. counterparts. But while political realities and the Japanese attitude may prevent such frankness, Americans should be aware that these sentiments thrive as an undercurrent that is slowly but surely rising to the surface.[19]

Japanese Foreign Investment in the United States:

For two generations after World War II, the United States was the world's foremost exporter of capital. Americans invested so heavily abroad that leaders of some nations feared a takeover by American capita. In the late 1960s French economist Jean-Jacques Servan Schriber even went so far as to predict that such American multinational corporations like IBM and ITT would turn Western Europe into an economic province ofthe United States.

By the 1980s, however, the tide had turned. Americans still continued to invest abroad in great numbers, but, unfortunately, the American economy continued to weaken. Years of huge budget and foreign trade deficits have led to a virtual collapse of the dollar. U.S. currency plunged some forty percent in value from 1985-87 against such major foreign currencies as the Japanese yen, the West German mark, and the British pound. The result is that American properties are going for unprecedented low prices because of the fall of the dollar. Thus, although the prices of American real estate and commercial properties seem high by American standards, they suddenly look very cheap to holders of other, stronger currencies.

Thus, one of the most pronounced trends in the American economy in recent years has been a tremendous growth in the amount of foreign investment. Foreign investment in the United States was about $1 trillion at the end of 1985. There are two types of foreign investment. The most obvious is about $167 billion of foreign direct investment which represents the purchase of such things as a factory or land. The rest of the money is in portfolio investments including corporate bonds, government securities, and common stock. Western Europe, with direct investments of about $107 billion in 1984, was the leader, distantly followed by Japan with $15 billion and Canada with $14 billion. Since that time there has been a substantial growth in Japanese investments.

Japan in the 1980s is rapidly becoming the world center for international finance and investment. For example, Japan's soaring yen and an explosion in equity prices has allowed Tokyo to outmuscle New York to become one of the world's largest stock markets. The capitalization of Nomura Securities Co. has alone ballooned to $54 billion, more than ten times that of Merrill Lynch & Co., the largest U.S. securities broker. Nomura's power is so massive and its financing so inexpensive that it has outpaced its Western rivals to become the leading underwriter in the huge market for Eurobonds.[20] Japan's four largest brokers, Nomura, Yamaichi, Nikko, and Daiwa, are also competing successfully against American brokers for a growing market share on Wall Street and by 1990 may be able to compete equally with Merrill Lynch and other American giants in New York as dealers in stocks and bonds.[21] Japan's brokers are doing to Wall Street what Japanese automobile manufacturers did to Detroit in the early 1970s.

In the late 1980s Japan has become the world's biggest capital exporting country and the world's largest creditor country. Japan's Ministry of Finance reported in June of 1987 that Japan's net foreign assets climbed to a record $180.4 billion at the end of 1986, making it the largest creditor nation for the second consecutive year. Net overseas assets increased 39 percent from the $129.8 billion recorded at the end of 1985, reflecting investment abroad of its huge trade surpluses.[22] That situation is in strong contrast to 1981, when the United States was the biggest creditor rather than one of the biggest debtors. At that time Japan's private sector had net liabilities of more than $18 billion. In 1986 U.S. net foreign liabilities increased to about $220 billion while Japan's net assets rose to $180 billion.[23]

The source of the capital for export is the Japanese people's immense savings. Consumers in Japan save 17% of their earnings against 4% in the United States. According to the Bank of Japan, their personal savings at the end of the 1986 fiscal year reached $3.8 trillion and total savings during that year grew by $352 billion, a growth rate of 17.6 percent.[24] The personal savings are largely concentrated in such things as insurance policies, investment trusts, trust bank instruments, public and corporate bonds, and postal savings accounts, and they are largely incorporated into the portfolios of institutional investors.[25]

In recent years within Japan, corporate demand for capital to invest in plants and equipment has become sluggish and asset management yields have dropped because of low interest rates. The result has been the rapid dispersion of international investment. For example, a glance at the portfolios of all Japan's major life insurance companies indicates that the ratio of foreign assets to total assets grew to 11.5 percent at the end of fiscal 1986, up sharply from 6.6 percent at the end of fiscal 1982. Specified money in trust and fund trusts managed in foreign securities by trust banks stood at only 25.5 billion yen, or 1 percent of the total assets managed in 1984, but this percentage had grown to 14.2 percent at the end of March, 1987. This is equal to a 12.8 fold increase in foreign investments by these banks in three short years.[26]

Bereft of enough investment opportunities at home to absorb their astonishing pile of savings, the Japanese are very anxious to find safe havens abroad to park their excess cash. The United States offers political and economic stability as well as higher interest rates to the foreign investor. Thus, Japan's investment in direct real estate and corporations reached $23.4 billion at the end of 1986 with the likelihood that Japanese investments could continue to grow at a continuously faster pace. A favorite Japanese target is America's skylines. By late 1987 they had invested an estimated $7 billion in office towers and other buildings.[27]

The fastest growing sector of foreign investment in the United States is the portfolio investment. Foreigners are attracted by high American interest rates. The Japanese, for example, have been greatly attracted by Treasury bills and bought up some $54.5 billion in 1985. This increased to

$60 billion in 1986, a year when Japanese investors eagerly pumped about $80 billion into American financial markets. In 1986 Japanese investors had purchased as much as 75 percent of the total Treasury bonds auctioned. For the past several years Japanese institutional investors have taken a steady 60-70 percent of auctioned Treasury bonds. Currently, these investors are footing about 25 percent to one third of the Reagan administration's huge budget deficit and if such investments were to cease, U.S. bond prices would slump as interest rates would rise.[28]

Indeed, it is the vast sums of money that foreigners are pouring into America's stock and bond markets that have had the greatest impact on the U.S. economy. In 1986 foreigners held more than $500 billion worth of U.S. Treasury and other government securities. The fact is that foreigners are supplying the funds that enable the United States to continue piling up its extravagant national debt. The U.S. has become a mega debtor like Brazil and Mexico.[29]

The Japanese are now beginning to move away from the safety of Treasury bonds, however, and there is evidence that they are becoming far more speculative with their money. There have been times when the Japanese have played a significant role in driving up the price of gold on New York's Commodity Exchange. Another significant target has been Wall Street. For every six months over the past two years, new Japanese investment in American stocks has doubled, reaching about $4 billion in late 1986. In the first three months of 1987, the Japanese bought $3.5 billion in U.S. stocks, which means that their purchase of American stocks reached a rate of four times greater than that of the previous year.

Japanese are buying great amounts of blue-chipstocks with American Express, Dow Chemical, Disney, Merrill Lynch, IBM, and Citicorp. Sears and First Chicago also showed big percentage increases between January 1986 and January 1987. The Japanese are third behind Great Britain and Switzerland in foreign equity investment in the U.S. The $17 billion that flowed in during the first nine months of 1986 was more than twice the total for 1985 and it is estimated that the Japanese could put at least $25 billion in U.S. equities in 1987.[30]

Japanese investors are also making huge inroads into American real estate. They invested only about $1 billion in 1984 in U.S. real estate, but by 1986 this figure had reached six billion.[31] Japanese targets are becoming increasingly grandiose and include a number of skyscrapers in New York. For example, recently Mitsui bought the Exxon building on Sixth Avenue for $610 million while Shuwa paid $175 million for the ABC headquarters only a few blocks away. Dai-Ichi acquired the Tiffany building on Fifth Avenue for $94 million. Zeckendorf Towers, a building complex near Union Square in New York, exists as a result of Kumagai Gumi's $1.2 billion commitment to a joint venture with William Zeckendorf, Jr.

Japanese investments have both helped and hurt the United States. Americans have benefited greatly from this inflow of portfolio investments since both the Federal government, as well as businesses and consumers, have access to capital that would not have otherwise been available without higher interest rates and taxes. On the other hand, this huge surge in portfolio investments has raised the value of the dollar, thus hurting attempts by the Reagan administration to redress the growing foreign trade gap.

Japanese insurance companies are also investing in the United States. Until recently, Japanese life insurers spent most of their huge pools of money at home. However, spurred by new pressures to offer their many policyholders higher rates of return, together with reduced economic growth in Japan and looser regulations, many Japanese life insurance companies have quickly begun to move money overseas. The industry's investment in foreign securities rose to 61 percent in 1986 to just under $50 billion in the fiscal year ended March 31, 1987, up from $31 billion in the fiscal year ended March 31, 1986.[32] Nippon Life, for example, had about $320 million invested in overseas stock markets at the end of the 1987 fiscal year with $207 million in American stocks, $53 million in West German companies, $20 million in British equity, and smaller amounts in Switzerland, the Netherlands, France, and Singapore.[33]

These insurance companies are just as conservative as many other Japanese companies investing in the United States. They have invested heavily in long-term United States Treasury bills, which offer them security and higher interest rates than those in Japan. They are such a force in this market that some U.S. investment firms state that they and other Japanese investors in Treasury bills have been able to move bond prices in the United States by hinting that they might refrain from buying in upcoming auctions. They are also stepping up purchases of real estate and equities.

American corporations are courting Japanese investors in order to gain access to their huge trade surplus of hundreds of billions of dollars. These American corporations are beginning to sop up the surplus dollars by selling their bonds in Japan. It is said that such firms as Standard Oil are lining up to sell $1.5 billion in bonds in the late 1980s and that they are offering higher interest rates than those on U.S. Treasury bonds.

Japanese Employment in the U.S.:

Today Japanese-owned companies have become employers of tens of thousands of Americans. There is an increased number of Japanese companies moving part of their operations to the United States, and a steadily growing number of Americans receive their livelihood from these Japanese firms. There is every indication that this trend will continue in the future.

It is clear that Japanese investment in various American production facilities has developed its own momentum. By the end of 1985 there were 405 American-based assembly or manufacturing companies in which Japanese investors owned a majority share. These companies had a total of 583 plants in operation, an increase of 70 in 1985 alone. The number of Japanese owned manufacturing plants in 1985 was almost double that of 1980.[34] California was by far the most popular site for Japanese plants in 1985 with 153 plants. Georgia was a very distant second with 37 plants followed by Texas, New Jersey, and Illinois, all of which had more than 30 Japanese affiliated plants each.[35] There were also significant numbers of Japanese companies in such Southeastern states as Tennessee, North Carolina, and South Carolina.

This increase in investment has also meant a substantial increase in employment of Americans. It is estimated that Japanese manufacturers employed about 100,000 Americans at the end of 1985 in industries ranging from metals and motor vehicles to communications and computer equipment. This is a significant increase over the 50,000 Americans employed by Japanese companies as recently as 1980.[36]

Much of the initial employment was attributed to the Japanese purchase of existing plant facilities by Japanese companies. Japanese firms would buy such things as an electronics plant in the United States and would use existing facilities and/or workers. There has been a distinct reversal of this trend, however. Japanese companies now tend to favor the practice of new construction. For example, Komatsu recently began construction of a new factory in Chattanooga.

Most of the Japanese concerns in the United States are medium in size, but recently a growing number of these operations qualify as big businesses in terms of sales, investment, and employment. Automobile manufacturers, such as the huge Honda plant in Marysville, Ohio, and consumer electronics industries are among the largest companies. The three largest of the Japanese automobile companies with facilities in the United States employed almost 7,000 workers in 1986, while the three largest consumer electronics employers had a total of about 6,200 workers at four plants. Other significant manufacturing sectors represented in the United States by Japanese companies include chemicals, foodproducts, metals and machinery.[37]

While Americans look favorably at increased employment opportunities, the trend toward locating Japanese companies in the U.S. is causing considerable criticism and concern in Japan. According to a recent study, it is estimated that Japanese corporations will have invested enough by the year 2000 to create 1.2 million jobs abroad, many of them in the United States. Americans complain when U.S. based corporations build factories in such places as Mexico to take advantage of cheaper labor. Now Japanese labor leaders are voicing the same complaint -- that the use of cheaper facilities abroad will cause increased unemployment at home.

Japanese firms build factories in the United States for a variety of reasons. Cost is certainly a factor. If a commodity, region, or state is willing to give significant tax holidays or reductions for a number of years, setting up an operation abroad can become quite economical. Furthermore, the cost of buying land and building new sites in Japan has become prohibitively expensive. Construction costs are comparatively less in the United States. The Japanese also like to build in the United States to save on the cost of shipping goods destined for the U.S. and to have closer access to natural resources such as iron ore and coal. One of the major problems facing Japanese companies at home is the skyrocketing increase in the price of fuel.

The growing Japanese economic presence in the United States has meant that many American communities are experiencing an influx of Japanese. Japanese corporations like to send their better employees abroad for two or more years and married workers often bring their families. The result is a new phenomenon -- the need for an American community to adjust to an influx of many Japanese. The following is the experience of a small city in the state of Tennessee.

The Japanese in Rutherford County, Tennessee:
A Case Study[38]

Tennessee, although a small state in population, ranks number one in the United States in direct Japanese investment. The thirty-six Japanese companies and $1.5 billion dollar investment in Tennessee in 1986 are concrete evidence of the economic effects of the internationalization of the economy upon one American state. This Japanese presence has had a great social and economic impact on several Tennessee communities.

Rutherford county is located in the geographic center of Tennessee and has an approximate population of 84,000. The county is 32 miles southeast of Nashville. Murfreesboro, the county seat of Rutherford County, had a population of 32,800 in 1980. LaVergne and Smyrna are two small towns in Rutherford County that are near Murfreesboro.

A large Japanese corporation famous for its automobile tires, Bridgestone, acquired a Firestone tire plant in LaVergne in 1983. In 1986 Bridgestone employed 861 workers, including 32 Japanese advisors. A Bridgestone official from Japan stated that his company chose the Firestone facility because "this area is in the central part of the United States. It is very convenient to deliver tires to all areas of the United States. And there was already an established plant here." Another Japanese official of Bridgestone noted that "the people who live in the countryside are more friendly, more honest, more diligent than the people who live in the city." There was also the feeling that there would be less crime in Tennessee than in New York, Los Angeles, or other large American cities.

American workers at the Firestone plant were also delighted with the 1983 Bridgestone takeover of their plant. An American manager stated:

> Firestone was in a position where with this plant and the product they produced, they were losing money and had intended and announced the closure of this plant. So, naturally our feeling when we found out that Bridgestone would be buying and taking over was very good.... I was looking forward to it because from what I had read and what I knew about successes that Japanese companies had, I expected their technology and their engineering ability to be very high and I was looking forward to that and being able to implement a lot of those things here in this plant.

After several years of working together, bothAmericans and Japanese have formed impressions of eachother as workers. An American manager stated:

> In relation to business I expected ... they would be perfectionists; that they had perfected their industry and their manufacturing techniques and I found that to be basically true.... I expected them to be very hard working -- long hours and a lot of devotion to the job.... I did find that to be exactly true.

A Japanese manager commented that the Americans worked very hard as individuals, but they did not perform as well when they were obliged to work together as a team.

When the Japanese took over, American managers were sent to Japan for intensive two-week training sessions. The major purpose of the trips was for the Americans to view quality circle activity in Japan to better understand Japanese working methods. The American workers have adopted a modified form of the quality circle concept that has been working in a satisfactory manner for both sides.

A potentially even more difficult task was the integration of the Japanese into a small Southern city. According to Sharon Summers, Director of Bilingual Services for Rutherford County Schools, however, the adjustment was quite easy for local residents. A nearby air force base meant that there was a constant stream of people coming through the city. As a result, the local population was used to new people moving into the community. Foreign students had studied at the local university for many years and several Vietnamese families had settled there at the end of the Vietnam War. Thus, a new group of foreigners in Murfreesboro was no great shock.

Japanese children, however, had problems adjusting to American schools. No one was speaking Japanese, and the Japanese students were suddenly bombarded with an alien language. Some of them just sat down and cried, but over time they all made a successful adjustment and became very happy. According to Sharon Summers:

> Some of the things that Japanese teenagers really enjoyed in the U.S.: They don't have to wear uniforms to school. They can dress in their jeans, which most of them basically wear each day.... The girls really like being able to have their hair cut, have perms, pierce their ears, they can wear more makeup.

One perceptive Japanese student noted:

> The first day it felt I missed Japan; it was awful. I couldn't talk English and it was a very long day. American schools' children have more freedom because we don't have much homework in American school. In Japanese schools teachers put more pressure on the students to make higher grades than the American school. In the American schools, the teacher doesn't put pressure on the students that much.

The major long-term problem facing Japanese students was the need to prepare for entrance exams for Japanese universities. Japanese corporations in general will only hire graduates of Japanese colleges and discriminate against Japanese with foreign degrees. Thus, it was necessary for Japanese students to keep up with their reading and writing skills and to study Japanese history and other subjects taught in Japanese high schools.

One solution to this problem has been the establishment of a special Saturday school staffed by volunteers from the Japanese community. All classes are in Japanese and students study both the Japanese language and advanced subjects. Other Japanese communities across the United States have also adopted the practice of Saturday schools.

Japanese adults made successful efforts to become active members of the community. Some of the Japanese men hunted, boated, and camped with their American colleagues. Japanese women became active in a variety of community projects. The only practice that one Japanese male refused was the chewing of tobacco. Few,if any, of the Japanese were clannish. A World War II veteran summed up the feelings of many of his American neighbors by noting:

> In World War II, I had to go over there and fight them. They sent a Kamikaze aboard us, (it) came right straight down and hit the after-deck of the ship. If they want to come in and act decent toward us, that's alright with me. They used to be our enemies; now they are our neighbors.

Promoting America: Efforts to Lure Japanese Business to the U.S.

Many American communities and states have attempted to attract Japanese corporations. Inducements include promises of tax abatements and good living conditions for Japanese. Some states have set up offices to promote the invitation of Japanese companies to their state. North Carolina, for example, established a North Carolina Japan Center which is active in bringing Japanese companies to the state, assisting North Carolinians who wish to work in Japan, and in promoting the study of Japanese culture, history, and language throughout North Carolina. Dr. Hiroko Kataoka, who teaches Japanese at North Carolina State University and is affiliated with the Center, has pioneered a very successful effort to spread the study of Japanese on many campuses throughout the Southeast.[39]

Vermont in Japan:

One does not readily think of a relationship between a major economic power like Japan and a tiny agricultural state like Vermont. Few Japanese I know had any real knowledge of Vermont -- most associated it with the name that the Japanese food products corporation chose for one of its curry mixes -- Vermont House Curry. Nevertheless, there is a growing relationship between the two entities and Vermont recently became the 33rd American state to set up a promotional office in Japan.

Traditionally there have been few people ororganizations with an interest specifically in Japan. The University of Vermont, St. Michael's College, and Middlebury College often offer courses on Japan, and Middlebury has long had an excellent institute for the study of Japanese during the summer. Each summer St.Michael's hosts a large contingent of Japanese students who come to study English. Other Vermont colleges sometimes offer courses on Japan.

There was a surge of interest in Japan in Vermont after the 1982 establishment of the Japan Society in Vermont by Alan Andrews, who teaches religion at the University of Vermont, Peter Corfin, a businessman who has lived in Japan for several years, and Takeo Iguchi, the newly appointed consul general in Boston. Frank Tenny, a retired foreign service officer who grew up and served in Japan for many years, provided the Society with added depth following his move to Vermont. The Society has had three main focuses: the arts, education, and business. Its many forums, conferences, exhibits, and guest speakers have sparked a greater awareness of Japan in the Green Mountain State.

Before Governor Madeleine Kunin and Development Agency Secretary James Guest went to Japan in 1985, there were already notable ties between the two states. IBM with its office in Burlington had long worked with the Japanese. The UST Corp., a Japanese business that makes steel chains and sprockets, opened a plant in Bennington in 1977 and employs 125 Vermonters. Over 100 Vermont companies have export contracts with Japanese partners.

Kunin's group worked closely with Sumitomo Industries, Japan's third largest conglomerate. The purpose of the trip was merely to begin the process of personal relations described in Chapter Three. The Vermonters, in trying to sell their state to the Japanese, noted that Vermont is ranked third nationally in terms of productivity, has the lowest record of absenteeism in the U.S., is ranked fourth in the percentage of workers in high tech, and has a superb record for quality education.

When Hosai Hyuga, chairman of Sumitomo Industries, came to the US in 1986 to present the commencement address at St. Michael's College, he brought a delegation of 13 Sumitomo officials who met a wide range of Vermonters. A later step was the opening of Vermont's Economic Development Office in Osaka in 1986. Interestingly, the office is funded by Sumitomo Metal Industries and directed by Mr. Koji Akizawa, a Kunin appointee who was head of Sumitomo-Intercom. According to James Guest:

> In his capacity as Liaison Officer, Mr. Akizawa's goal is to encourage one or more of the Sumitomo companies to locate a facility in Vermont and to promote Vermont to other expansion-minded Japanese businesses and promote the development of tourism and trade between Japan and Vermont.[40]

It is too early to discuss the successes or failures of this office, but Sumitomo's willingness to fund it greatly enhances the possibility of success.

The Danger of Japan Bashing:

In American political circles today, Japan "bashing" has become very fashionable. The U.S. trade deficit continues at a record pace and Japan now accounts for almost 40 percent of it. The Japanese have promised to stimulate domestic consumption and to open their markets, but their pattern of timely promise and untimely performance has cost them credibility. Furthermore, there are many Americans who still remember World War II and who have difficulty in adjusting to the idea of Japan as an ally. Many Americans were annoyed by the case of Toshiba's selling highly sensitive military equipment to the Soviet Union in 1987. Would an ally behave in such a way?

Richard Darman, former Deputy Secretary of the Treasury has outlined four basic problems with Japan "bashing."[41] First, it will not fix our trade deficit or cause savings-oriented Japanese to start consuming like Americans. The Japanese are rapidly increasing their consumption of American goods, but it is not realistic to think that the Japanese will stop purchasing their own goods for American products. Japanese industry provides the Japanese with most of what they need. Further Japan "bashing" will only further alienate the Japanese from America and increase the chance of destructive economic "warfare."

Secondly, current Japan "bashing" foolishly focuses on Japanese manufacturing trade. In reality, however, our current-account deficit reflects a broader set of problems. It extends beyond Japan to Europe, Canada, and other states in Asia and includes such matters as increased international competition in investment and services. We need a broader view of international trade and finance.

The third problem with Japan "bashing" is that it distracts Americans from attending to basic domestic problems. It may make us more comfortable to blame others for our troubles, but such an attitude makes us less inclined to examine our own shortcomings:

> There are many ways to become more competitive without depending upon foreign action. We need to reduce the fiscal deficit; increase investment in applied civilian R&D; encourage more efficient and entrepreneurial corporate management; raise productivity, especially in the service sector; restore the value of the work ethic, and radically improve our lagging education system by making far better use of technology and increasing the average school year. It is now 180 days in the U.S. vs. 240 in Japan. Such actions amount to a policy of constructive -- not destructive -- unilateralism. But they all have evident costs. So it is natural that our political system would welcome an excuse to avoid facing up to them. Japan "bashing" provides just such an excuse.[42]

Japan-bashing is also foolish foreign policy. Our foreign policy goals must be to preserve the peace while expanding market-oriented democracy. One cannot expand power today through nuclear weapons and conventional military forces. While these act as a stabilizing deterrence, the key to expansion of power and influence today is in trying to shape the emerging world through aid, trade, investment, and technology transfer. Economic strength provides a peaceful basis for accomplishing these goals.

From this perspective Japan must be considered a strategic superpower. Its GNP is greater than that of the Soviet Union, twice that of Germany, and 3.5 times that of Great Britain. And with its extraordinary savings rate, it is accumulating huge trade surpluses that it can distribute around the world as it sees fit.

Many American politicians are urging the rearmament of Japan, but this would cause a new arms race in Asia, insecurity in a region that has bad memories of Japanese militarism, and would make little economic sense. Wasting time and energy to build a questionable military is not in our mutual interests. Our goal must be to assure that Japan's economic power is used to advance market-oriented democracy.

Conclusion:

Very few Americans outside of the business world are aware of the fact that Japan has suddenly emerged as the nerve center of the financial world and that it is using vast amounts of money to prop up many aspects of the American economy, including the Treasury bond market. It is clear that some Americans blame their woes on the Japanese and are calling for more controls over the importation and usage of Japanese finance. Other more desperate families and communities seek greater access to this money. Japan's success in finance may well lead to a decline in U.S.-Japanese relations as a new wave of nationalism is sweeping Japan. The economies of the two nations are so interdependent that a breakdown in relations could have a devastating impact on the economies of both nations.

CHAPTER VI - NOTES

1.   Daniel Burstein, "America's Debt, Japan's Leverage," *The New York Times* (30 April 1987), p. A31.

2.   *Ibid.*

3.   Interview with Akira Tsukamoto, August 17, 1987, in Tokyo. Tsukamoto is a reporter for Nihon Terebi in Tokyo.

4.   R. Z. Aliber, "US-Japanese Economic Relationships," in M. Kaplan et .al., eds., *Japan, American and the Future World Order* (New York: Heath, 1976), p. 225.

5.   *Time* (12 April 1987), p. 32.

6.   *Ibid.*

7.   *Ibid.*

8.   *Japan Economic Survey* (July 1986), p. 2.

9.   *The New York Times* (6 June 1987), p. 1.

10.   The results of this poll are in marked contrast to the results of a poll of Koreans published in the 30 March 1987 issue of *The Korea Herald*. According to this poll of 21,166 Koreans, the United States is the most favored country while Japan is the least-liked nation.

Favorite Nation		Least Favorite Nation	
United States	31.8%	Japan	41.6%
Britain	19.1%	Soviet Union	33.2%
Switzerland	16.9%	China	9.0%
France	15.9%	United States	6.1%
West Germany	7.0%	East Germany	2.5%
Japan*	2.5%		

*11th place

11.   Burstein, p. A31.

12.   *Time*, p. 32.

13.   The Japan Economic Institute of America, *U.S.-Japan Economic Relations Yearbook 1984-1985* (Washington: JEI, 1986), pp. 103-115.

14.   *Ibid.*

15.   *Ibid.*

16.   *Ibid.*

17.   *Mitsubishi Bank Review* (June 1987), p. 1033.

18.   *Ibid.*

19.   Masahiko Ishizuka, "The Real Cause of the U.S. Trade Deficit," *Nihon Keizai Shimbun* (17 January 1987).

20.   *Business Week* (13 July 1987), p. 57.

21.   *Business Week* (7 September 1987), p. 83.

22.   *Japan Economic Survey* (July 1987), p. 3.

23.   *Ibid.*

24.   "Timid Giants -- Japanese Institutional Investors", *Tokyo Business Today* (August 1987), p. 43.

25.   There is less need for Americans to save quite as much as Japanese. Americans receive far more social benefits than the Japanese. For example, social security payments are much higher in the United States. Paying for these programs is a kind of forced savings that does not appear on the ledgers of savings banks.

26.   *Ibid.*, p. 44.

27.   "For Sale: America," *Time* (14 September 1987), p.55.

28.   *Ibid.*, p. 42.

29.   In the late 1980s the U.S. debt increased at a great pace. In 1986 the U.S. sent overseas a net $10 billion in the form of interest, dividends, and rent. By 1990 the United States will ship $50 billion to the Japanese, Germans, British, and other foreign creditors. Source: *Business Week* (16 November 1987), p. 160.

30.   *Business Week* (March 1987), p. 27-28.

31.   Daniel Burstein, "Rising sun on Wall Street," *New York Magazine* (2 March 1987), p. 32-33.

32.   *The New York Times* (3 August 1987), p. 23.

33.   *Ibid.*

34.   *Japan Economic Survey*, XI. 2 (February 1987), p.16.

35. *Ibid.*

36. *Ibid.*

37. *Ibid.*

38.   Lucien Ellington and Richard Rice, eds., "Intercultural Contact: The Japanese in Rutherford County, Tennessee," in *The Occasional Papers of the Virginia Consortium for Asian Studies*, IV (1987), pp.26-34.   This is the narrative of a 30-minute video that was shown on Educational Television in Tennessee.

39.   Other states have set up offices in Tokyo to attract Japanese investment. Virginia, for example, has a large suite of offices in Tokyo which in 1984 was run by a Japanese businessman who had recently retired from the Bank of Tokyo.

40.   James Guest, "Doing Business with Japan," in *Vermont Affairs*, op. cit., p. 7.

41.   Richard G. Darman, "What's wrong with Japan bashing," *U.S. News & World Report* (5 October 1987), pp.53-54.

42. *Ibid.*

CHAPTER VII

TRADING AND MARKETING WITH THE JAPANESE

No study of Japanese business can be complete without a few comments on the nation's foreign trade. Japan's growing volume of foreign trade and its huge trade surplus vis-a-vis the United States has made news headlines since the early 1970s. Unfortunately, there have been several myths and misconceptions concerning Japanese foreign trade.

The Japanese Customer Today

Writers in *Business Week* recently noted a substantial change among Japanese consumers and concluded that upper-middle class Japanese today are getting far higher salaries and are abandoning their thrifty ways in favor of increased personal spending:

> Yuko Shimizu is 32 and owns a $138,000 condominium on Tokyo's fashionable West Side. She plays tennis weekly, paying court fees that approach $45 an hour, and has recently joined a horseback-riding club. Saturday sewing lessons, a night-school course, and season tickets to the symphony round out her busy schedule. All told, she earns about $32,000 a year as an administrative assistant at a Tokyo think tank. Even after paying for all those goodies, she is still left with $625 a month in pocket money.
>
> So whatever happened to Japanese workaholics who salted away every spare yen? They're still around, but more and more Japanese in their 20s and early 30s are leading lives similar to Shimizu's. Says one just-married 27-year old who earns $25,000 a year: "We don't plan to save." Paradoxically, he works for Japan's Finance Ministry, which has long fostered policies that discourage consumption and encourage a household savings rate that still exceeds 16% of disposable income.[1]

This trend is still largely confined to Tokyo and to unmarried people, but fatter paychecks have enabled the Japanese to live far more lavishly than their parents did. The average worker's monthly take-home pay rose to $2,337 per household in 1985, a real increase of 33% from 1971. The Japanese are also altering their traditional spending patterns. Grocery purchases are only 1.7% higher then in 1971 while restaurant spending has soared by 36%, and the amount spent on leisure activities has shot up 32%.[2]

American marketers in Japan must realize that these trends reflect more than a shift in Japanese consumer spending; they indicate a revolution in lifestyle. The younger Japanese consumer no longer wants to have a lot of possessions or to "keep up with the Tanakas." Now the money is spent on things that will stress his individuality. Following the U.S. model, Japanese "yuppies" and would-be "yuppies" are spending to achieve a uniqueness -- a slice of life different from anybody else.

Older Japanese decry the current shift in generational attitudes. Parents now worry about the breakup of the extended family, and employers are starting to complain that workers are not loyal. They are correct -- younger Japanese are out to enjoy life. Many are opting for jobs that give them greater freedom to spend time as they choose. They seem to want to stay single longer and to have plenty of money to spend.

Younger Japanese are now accustomed to using credit cards at will and the preference of spending over saving has taken root. According to one survey, working singles in Tokyo earn in excess of $1,200 on average a month plus an annual bonus of $3,300. Monthly fixed living expenses -- saving, housing and utilities -- average more than $430 and personal spending comes to $565.[3] Young female office workers, "OLS or office ladies," are among the biggest spenders. Although they may only earn $13-14,000 a year, they get around costs for room and board by living with parents. Thus, a Tokyo secretary with a $13,000 a year salary can set aside up to a third of her salary and all bonus money.

Per capita gross national product in Japan now exceeds that of the United States by a growing margin. The Japanese have a great deal of money to spend and are very much in a spending mood.

Japanese Foreign Trade

Foreigners commonly believe that Japan is totally dependent on foreign trade for its economic survival and that its postwar growth has been propelled by trade. There is also the belief that Japan's economy has been export led and that production for export is the primary occupation of

Japanese industry. These arguments and others like them often stem from European and American pressure groups that are threatened by Japanese competition. There is little truth to these beliefs.

Foreign trade plays a comparatively minor role in Japan's economy; the role of exports and imports in total output is surprisingly low. Recent figures show that Japan's share of foreign trade as a percentage of its total GNP is well below that of virtually all Western industrial powers. Only the United States has a smaller percentage. Thus, although Japan is the world's greatest importer of raw materials and one of the major exporters of manufactured goods, in overall terms it is less of a trading nation than many European states.

Japan's economic growth after World War II was fueled by the domestic market. Trade barriers made it hard for foreigners to export their wares in Japan. Thus, when Sony produced its first tape recorders in the 1950s, it did not have to compete with foreign tape recorders; it had the market to itself. Since many Japanese wanted tape recorders in the 1950s, Sony grew quickly.

Trade dependence has only risen at a small rate through time despite more than a twenty-fold increase in trade from 1955-75. The overall increase of Japanese trade in terms of the total growth of world trade has been less than that of many modern industrial nations such as the United States and the Soviet Union. The major reason for this development in Japan can be attributed to the following:

> The spread of growth implied that, fast as exports developed, total output more or less kept pace. The nature of growth, set as it was on manufacturing, meant that the need for finished imports were never really large, while needs for raw material imports hardly increased, thanks to import saving production processes and shifts in consumer demand away from import sensitive commodities.[4]

The structure of Japanese foreign trade is quite different from that of other large industrial nations. Japan has a very asymmetrical and unique commodity composition of foreign trade flows -- an overwhelming though declining share of raw materials for imports and a large and increasing share of manufactured items in exports. This fact reflects the lack of natural

resources on the Japanese islands and the competitiveness and quality of
Japanese manufactured goods.

American criticism has focused on Japan's dependence on export
markets for continued economic growth without in turn providing a market
for manuˆfactured goods from the United States in Japan. "Japan's export
dependence is often minimized as being asmall percentage of GNP, but this
misses the point;exports are almost exclusively manufactured (96%+) and
represent 30% or more of production for certain key industries like steel,
shipbuilding and automobiles...the rancor and tensions are not due too much
to the aggregate export level, but rather, export concentration in a few
products."[5] The American response should not be one of complaints and
protectionism, but, rather, one of improved production by American
industries most affected by Japanese exports (eg., the construction of better,
smaller cars).

Foreign Trade and Growth

The relationship between foreign trade and economic growth is highly
complex and well beyond the scope of this work. Nevertheless, a few aspects
of the problem are worthy of discussion. Rapp and Feldman note:

> Exports were an important source and support to
> growth in the postwar era. In volume terms, export markets
> provided the sales prospects to justify continued large capital
> equipment expenditures once an industry was established
> domestically. Firms expanded into foreign markets and
> increased their competitiveness through additional investment,
> higher productivity, and more sales, which at the same time
> lowered domestic prices and bolstered demand at home.
> Export dynamics thus represented a logical extension of
> domestic competition. As domestic markets developed first,
> Japan's shifting industrial structure translated with some lag
> into a shifting export structure. This phenomenon is
> sometimes called product cycle evolution.[6]

Imports have also played an important role in Japan's economic
growth. However, there has been a change in the nature of the link over
time. In prewar days imports provided Japan with highly necessary
technological equipment and new products that allowed Japan to keep pace
with technological progress abroad. Now, however, Japan is very advanced

technologically and no longer depends on the West as much for research and development.   The essential role of imports is not to lead industrial development, but, rather, to give it the necessary raw materials Japan cannot supply itself.

The interrelationship between Japanese exports and growth are far more complex. To be sure, exports are essential because Japan's borrowing capacity to pay for imports has never been great. In some respects, export spay for imports. This statement, however, does not answer the question of whether the primary stimulus for growth came from the domestic or from the export side. On the surface, it looks as though Japan's economy has been export-led, but some studies by economists have ledto the conclusion that "growth-led" exports are the key. They conclude that Japan's rate of growth of exports has been high because the rate of growth of its economy -- and its industrial sector in particular -- has been great. Exports are very much a result of domestic growth.[7]

Foreign Investment and Japan

The inability of foreign firms and countries to make capital investments in Japan over much of the postwar era has also been a source of friction. It was only in the 1970s that direct investment, both inward and outward from Japan, began to have some impact on the evolution of the Japanese economy.[8]

Before Japan began to have a regular balance of trade surplus in the 1960s, the Japanese government maintained rigorous exchange controls to prevent capital outflows. Capital inflows were also closely regulated so that the foreign debt could be kept at a minimum. In the 1960s Japan was a net debtor, but only by a tiny amount. By 1967 a regular surplus was achieved and Japan had become a net creditor.

Foreign investment in Japan has been increasing in recent years due to steps to liberalize capital movements. It is clear that net foreign earnings will be making a major contribution to Japan's balance of payments in the future, thus obviating the need for trade surplus. Despite these recent developments, however, it is unlikely that the Japanese government will endorse, even in principle, the idea of the freedom of capital movement of all types.

Direct Investment

While direct investments have not represented a very large portion of Japan's international assets or liabilities, they have been a very controversial form of financial involvement with the rest of the world. These investments have been very strictly regulated throughout the postwar era:

> The reason that direct investment has received so much attention is that it involves the total transplanting of foreign enterprise, including its entrepreneurs, technology and marketing skills, as well as capital. Japanese distrust of foreigners with its deep historical roots was undoubtedly a crucial element in setting the restrictive tone of Japan's attitudes toward foreign enterprise in Japan.
>
> The control of foreign investment was laid down in 1950 through the Law Concerning Foreign Investment. The Law was intended to protect Japanese-owned firms from foreign competition. Foreign investment was permitted only when it helped achieve Japanese self-sufficiency and thereby contributed to overcoming the balance of payments deficit. Foreign firms were permitted at most 49% ownership of Japanese enterprises. Over time a number of changes were introduced into the controls, which culminated in a series of five rounds of liberalization. Under the fifth round of liberalization of 1 May 1973, foreigners could obtain 100 percent ownership of Japanese enterprises, subject to certain exceptions...."[9]

Marketing In Japan

Before entering the Japanese market, the American businessman needs to formulate a coherent and workable marketing plan and should select an agent in Japan to work on his behalf. American businessmen will find that the United States Department of Commerce in Washington or one of its regional offices is a useful resource inplanning marketing strategies.[10]

Developing a Marketing Plan

Every American company with a serious interest in the Japanese market should first establish a marketing plan. More assured results are obtained when a study and recommendation have been made by a market research firm or a business consultant, not by the Japanese agent. However, both the Japanese agent and the U.S. company should be consulted throughout the preparation of the plan.

The marketing plan should establish the location and size of the potential market for American products. This means that the plan should pinpoint where comparable products are being sold and in what numbers; for example, what percentage are sold in department stores, specialty stores, chain stores, superstores, self-service stores, and neighborhood stores.

Market location also means that the characteristics of the potential customer should be defined since the buying audience in Japan is often different than that in the United States and has different expectations. The American marketer must know the characteristics of potential Japanese consumers in terms of age, sex, educational level, occupation, hobbies, and interests. He must know where these people normally shop. Do Japanese in the late 1980s still shop in their own immediate neighborhoods? He should also know the geographical location of the potential markets. Is it primarily confined to urban areas, or should the rapidly expanding suburbs and outlying rural areas also be included?

The marketing plan should show market distribution and provide objectives and timetables. How comparable goods are distributed in Japan should be examined. Do they go direct to major retailers or must they pass through a wholesaler? Who are the potential wholesalers and retailers who will handle the products? The marketing plan should also provide short and long-term timetables and objectives for establishing distribution to the potential market. Obviously, establishing distribution channels in Japan takes time, and most agents do not have the capability to move goods quickly through the entire potential market. Therefore, this timetable should spell out the goals for reaching the market both in terms of sales outlets and geographical areas. As an example, the market plan could call for establishing distribution to Tokyo department stores in the first year; Osaka area department stores, Tokyo suburban department stores, and Tokyo major specialty stores in the second year; and Tokyo and Osaka wholesalers, and other major city department stores in the third year.

American businessmen generally will find such a study and plan to be a worthwhile investment, as it forces both the U.S. exporter and the Japanese agent to set forth an agreed-upon plan for promoting the product. It is particularly useful to the U.S. company to ensure that the Japanese agent is marketing the goods in a way that meets the objectives of the U.S. company.[11]

Selecting an Agent

Some U.S. companies have entered the Japanese market by establishing a wholly owned subsidiary or joint venture. However, the size of the investment and the time required to establish an effective distribution system have led most U.S. firms to utilize import agents. With few exceptions, essentially all U.S. consumer products sold in Japan are handled by agents.

Select an agent who already has established channels in the same or related product areas. Many Tokyo agents do not distribute outside of the Tokyo area, thus leaving 75 percent of the Japanese market uncovered. Instead of giving nationwide rights to a trading company dealing in a single region, the U.S. company should consider appointing agents in other major markets like Osaka, Kobe, Nagoya, Fukuoka, Sapporo, and Naha (Okinawa). A World Traders Data Report (WTDR) requested through the U.S. Department of Commerce or prepared by the American Embassy can help determine a potential agent's effectiveness and the area of Japan that a specific agent may cover. American companies should have a clear and firm agreement with their Japanese agents on how and where the products will be sold. Many Japanese agents follow a low volume, high margin marketing strategy towards imported goods, so the importance of having such an agreement cannot be underestimated.

U.S. manufacturers wishing to successfully enter the Japanese market must follow sound marketing practices. These should include offering a salable product, devising a sound marketing plan, and pledging long-term commitment to execute it. Companies that take other than a well-planned disciplined approach when entering the Japanese market may find the results to be very disappointing.

The region of the country to be penetrated and the age group of potential buyers can be important factors in entering the Japanese market. First, it should be noted that in Japan there is an "awareness factor." Knowledge of products that are new and/or innovative increases among those who are younger, more highly educated, and live in urban areas. For example, a study of consumer behavior in Japan conducted in the early 1970s by the Prime Minister's Office showed those who said they noticed and like reading advertisements were younger and more educated. The study also showed that the degree of willingness to use new products is a function of youth, education, and urbanity. Since the leading companies generally tend to be the longest established in their product lines, one can expect that the market-share of the "number one" company in each product line will increase as a function of distance from urban centers; conversely, the market share of the number two and three companies can be expected to increase as age decreases, educational level increases, and as we move towards urban areas. Therefore new products are often best introduced to young people in urban areas.

Supporting Your Agent

It is important for the U.S. company to offer sufficient financial incentives to the agent to motivate him to carry out the marketing plan. Many Japanese agents complain that they must buy from the U.S. company at the same price as sold to U.S. wholesalers and retailers. Generally, U.S. firms do not adjust their foreign market price downward, even though the costs of U.S. domestic advertising, administration, and sales have been eliminated. The agent must incur these costs in Japan, so it is important that U.S. companies rationally adjust their prices to maintain competition in the foreign market.

A U.S. company should also consider providing at least initial financial assistance to the Japanese agent to cover costs of advertising and sales promotion incurred in introducing the U.S. products in Japan. This is especially important if the Japanese agent is expected to expand his present distribution channels. In any case, it is important for the U.S. company to have a prior agreement with the agent that certain incentives and marketing support will be provided in accordance with the marketing plan. It is entirely possible that if this is not agreed upon beforehand and followed up by the U.S. firm, the Japanese agent will market the products in a way that is more profitable to him.

The Agent-Pricing Problem and Traditional Restrictive Practices

Earlier, the idea was introduced that a submarket for foreign goods already exists in Japan. This idea recently has been enhanced by Prime Minister Nakasone's highly publicized campaign in Japan for "buying American." Another way of describing this is to say that Japan is a ready-made, "instant" market consisting of prosperous and/or foreign-oriented persons, and that little market promotion is needed to reach these people. But this submarket is a limited market, and it serves the interests of the importer, wholesaler, and retailer more than it does those of the foreign manufacturer. It is more suited to prestigious, luxury items than it is to mass market U.S. products.

Some American businessmen have recorded substantial earnings domestically by selling large volumes of goods at low margins; however, profit in Japan on sales of imported goods, including U.S. products, traditionally has been on the basis of low volume and large profit margins. This precedent in the sale of foreign products continues throughout Japan. Importer, distributer, wholesaler, and retailer are all accustomed to handling limited quantities of a product at high profit margins. Everyone profits in this arrangement except the foreign manufacturer, often because many foreign companies are content to turn over the marketing of their products to an agent and then sit back and wait for the orders.

Until October 1972, the Japanese Trademark Law indirectly allowed the Japanese importer to set the selling price of imported products at whatever he wished. High prices frequently were set to avoid price competition with domestic products. The holder of the registered trademark in Japan, i.e., the importer, was allowed by Japanese Customs to import products bearing the trademark. The importer was often the same distributor for competitive Japanese products and was therefore interested in keeping the prices of imports high.

A too-often repeated axiom of doing business in Japan is "don't join up with the big trading companies -- find somebody small." Most small trading companies do not have the distribution system necessary to market goods successfully on an nationwide basis. Many of these importers have sales outlets only in a few department and specialty stores. The fact is, the size of the company is not as important as whether the agent has the resources and motivation to market the products to the expectations of the foreign company. In short, does the agent have appropriate distribution channels to "move" the product?

One of Japan's largest trading companies is also one of the leading distributors of U.S. processed food in Japan; Kentucky Fried Chicken has teamed up with Mitsubishi for a very successful partnership throughout Japan in the mid-1980s. Other large trading companies have distribution channels among food wholesalers and retailers.

Japanese department stores traditionally have prevented importers from expanding their distribution channels to other sales outlets. In the early days of the Meiji period, the department stores and trading companies sent buying missions overseas to bring back foreign goods to sell to the foreign residents of Japan and the rich Japanese. Of course, in those days there were very few outlets where foreign goods could be purchased. Today it is not infrequent for some department stores to flex their economic muscle and tell the smaller wholesalers and agents that they will buy the foreign products offered only on the condition that the agent does not sell it to their competitors.

Assume that a foreign company starts applying pressure on his Japanese agent to sell more and extend his distribution channels to other retail outlets and other parts of Japan. In most cases, the agent will go in the red. As long as the agent restricts his distribution only to that historic, ready-made submarket for imported goods, his costs will be low and his margin high. The volume of each product handled is small. If he wants to expand his business, he must handle many different product lines. As a result, most small importers are constantly looking for new products to sell. Most of the trade opportunity requests for consumer products received by the U.S. Embassy and Consulates in Japan are from such importers.

Working Towards an Understanding of Japanese Tastes

The majority of Japanese consumers are conservative. They are often suspicious of foreign products and would prefer to use a domestic product in its place. For many items, the foreign product is purchased as a novelty item and is not taken too terribly seriously. The Johnny Walker Black Label scotch will sit on the executive's shelf to impress his clients, but he will normally drink a domestic brew such as Suntory whiskey.

American businessmen must be aware of these matters before they can successfully sell their goods in any part of Japan. Consider these examples. Coffee in the United States is usually packaged in red, blue, or green. In Japan it is only packaged in black or gold. When an American coffee company in Japan changed its label from red to black and gold and launched a new ad campaign, it tripled its sales in two months. In the United States, tableware, dinnerware, and glassware usually come packaged in multiples of four for four, eight, or twelve persons. In Japan four is often considered an unlucky number, and Japanese sets come five to the box. In choosing their Western-style clothing, Japanese use the same criteria they have used for generations in choosing a kimono -- the type, texture, and quality of the material as well as workmanship. Except among the younger generation, style is not as important a consideration as it is in the United States. These are just a sampling of the indigenous marketing practices that differ from those in the United States. Many American companies have not looked for these differences and have made only moderate sales as a result.[12]

Successful marketing in Japan depends on a company's ability to adapt products to meet the preferences, customs, and requirements of the customer, as well as the regulations of the local government. Packaging changes may be necessary, and sales methods may need revision. In addition, advertising must be designed to meet the customs and expectations of consumers in the country in order to compete with local and other foreign brands. According to many Japanese sources, the usual response of an American manufacturer to a Japanese buyer requesting product adaptation is, "if the order is big enough, I'll make the changes." Japanese companies, on the other hand, make the changes BEFORE they enter the market, looking toward developing the market to the extent that sales gradually will amortize the cost of such changes.

Japan's success in overseas markets has been attributed to the vague concept of "Japan, Inc." This is defined as close government-business cooperation to divide up overseas markets and ensure that Japanese companies do not compete in the same markets. This explanation, however, avoids recognition of the fact that the Japanese companies compete ferociously for sales within the same overseas markets. The sales pitches by Isuzu and Mitsubishi in 1987 are designed to coax Americans away from their Hondas and Toyotas.

Since their first overseas trade in the 1860s, the Japanese have been learning how to develop and modernize their country. Today, the Japanese still seek further ways to continue that development. They conduct extensive research to determine what to sell overseas, what modifications are necessary, and what subtle marketing strategies should be used. For example, some Japanese automakers maintain full-time personnel in the United States who keep abreast of American preferences in automobile colors, upholstery style, design and other criteria. Japanese color television manufacturers make sets not only for different voltages, but also for the various types of color transmission systems used around the world.

Americans and Japanese have different attitudes towards buying foreign made goods. One of the keys to the modern success of the Japanese economy is the fact that the Japanese are loyal to domestically produced goods. They provide a ready-made mass market for Japanese manufacturers who are then not so dependent on foreign purchasers. However, many Americans buy products because they are well-made rather than because they are American made. Anderson, Indiana, for example, has several factories affiliated with General Motors. In the early 1980s when GM was laying off many workers, it was ironic to walk through the factory parking lots in Anderson and find that one car out of five was Japanese made. Some factory workers wrote letters to the *Anderson Daily News* to complain about their colleagues' purchases of Japanese cars. These writers claimed that it was the success of Japanese autoworkers in the United States that was causing such high unemployment in Detroit, Anderson, and elsewhere. A few GM workers with Japanese cars wrote back to say that they bought Japanese cars for their "superior quality." Their concern was with the quality and price of their personal automobile, and they would only buy the car best suited for their individual needs.

The United States is an individual-oriented culture. Thus, campaigns to persuade Americans to buy only domestically produced goods will probably not succeed. Japan, however, is a group-oriented society and the Japanese are more easily persuaded to buy Japanese-made goods first. One exception may be young people, who may find it prestigious to buy "foreign."

Retailing in Japan

Americans selling in Japan should have some knowledge of its highly complex retailing system. It is important to know, for example, that while many foreign goods can be purchased in small neighborhood stores, department stores and other large retail outlets in major cities are the major sources for foreign products. For most American marketers in Japan, it might be wise to concentrate on these larger stores after determining what product sells in what kind of store.

Department Stores

Japanese department stores are a marvel. The typical department store is 10 to 12 stories high with several layers of basements. One can enter these stores and buy almost anything imaginable. A full range of food products from exotic caviar to locally produced vegetables can be found on the basement floors. Besides offering a tremendous diversity of products, the upper floors feature a wide variety of restaurants, small amusement parks, schools (for housewives interested in cooking, crafts, etc.), barbershops and hairdressers. Many department stores have good bookstores. Tokyo and Osaka department stores are generally crowded and have impressive sales volumes.

Department stores frequently carry a wide variety of foreign products, including many luxury items. As a result, department stores are the most important outlet for American products; however, unfortunately, on a store-by-store basis, the sales volume of American goods is often limited. Thus, it is important for the American firm to establish distribution channels with as many department stores and department store chains as possible. It is important to note that while most department stores are regionally based, a number of Tokyo-Osaka-Nagoya firms have moved to other parts of the country.

Specialty Stores

While department stores have been in existence in one form or another for over 300 years, a new and very important participant in Japan's retail system is the specialty store. As their name implies, they specialize in the sale of one type of product made by a variety of manufacturers. These stores are becoming increasingly important sales outlets for such products as fashion goods, sporting goods, recordings, books, toys, and do-it-yourself and home improvement items. There are many specialty store chains that facilitate the spread of foreign goods. In addition, many individually owned specialty stores are accessible through major wholesalers.

Superstores

Superstores are another phenomenon that have caught on in recent years. They represent a cross between Americanstyle discount houses and large supermarkets. They are large volume, small margin stores that now account for more than ten percent of all retail sales in Japan (the same volume as department stores). Predictably, half their sales are food products while consumer durable and some nondurables account for the rest. Foreign goods are now being introduced including U.S. brandname merchandise, and these stores will become increasingly important as sales outlets for U.S. goods.

Supermarkets

Within the last two decades, small supermarkets have sprung up in many neighborhoods. They are usually only half the size of their American counterparts, but they do sell a wide variety of goods. The main difference is that Japanese supermarkets deal primarily with food products while American supermarkets also sell soaps, paper products, newspapers, and countless other non-food products that are found in other neighborhood stores. Except for very limited imported foods, supermarkets are not important outlets for foreign foods.

Neighborhood Stores

In the late 1970s Japan had roughly 1.61 million retail outlets, slightly more than the total number of retail outlets in the United States even though Japan has only half the population of the United States and is only the size of California. The vast majority of these outlets are neighborhood stores. They are generally very small by American standards and specialize in one kind of product (umbrellas, electronics, fruit, drugs/medicines, etc.). They have small sales volumes and carry only a very limited inventory. These stores serve as outlets for perishables, such as health and beauty preparations, as well as such items as stationery and inexpensive furniture. Recently small general stores that stay open for long hours, like the 7-11 store chain in the United States, have come into fashion. In fact, one can find actual 7-11 stores throughout Japan.[13]

These neighborhood stores are not very important when it comes to sales of foreign goods. Indeed, their importance has been grossly overstated. One can reach most of one's buying potential through department and specialty stores without the added cost and bother of trying to establish distribution channels with small neighborhood outlets.

Other Retailing Methods

Mail order and door-to-door sales are rare in Japan and should not even be contemplated by foreign sellers.

The Japanese Distribution System

Many foreigners complain that the Japanese distribution system is so complex that it is impossible for an American to penetrate the market. Despite this certainly natural reaction, the complexity of marketing goods in Japan can be overcome with hard work, patience, and study. Some American firms have made breakthroughs and have managed to sell their products in great numbers.

The Japanese distribution system is far too difficult to discuss here in detail, but it is important to note that it is highly fragmented. Thus, the small producer and small retailer are very dependent on a number of wholesalers for transport, storage, sales promotion, the granting of credit, and the absorption of risk through the sales of items on a consignment basis. To serve all these small producers and retailers, a great number of wholesalers and a complex wholesaling system are needed.

Japan is a nation of small stores and small producers. One always reads about the big companies and department stores in Tokyo and Osaka, but it is the growing number of small "mom and pop" operations (four or less workers) where most Japanese shop on a daily basis. Both small retailers and producers need wholesalers to act as intermediaries for many reasons. The producer needs capital and funds and can use the wholesaler as a kind of banker who can prepay him for others or give him important raw materials. The wholesaler also acts as shipper, sales promoter, and storer of goods. This allows the small producer to concentrate on production alone. The average retailer is very small in retail sales and in size. He needs the wholesaler to store his goods, deliver them, and to delay payment of goods until their sale. In recent years, the size of producers has been growing slowly and they have been able to rationalize their distributions somewhat. However, there remains a large number of retailers, and the need for a wholesaler to assemble a wide variety of goods for a tiny store is very great.

As has been indicated in this chapter, the number of larger stores is rising slowly. Supermarkets, superstores, and department stores can be found in most urban areas in greater numbers than even in the 1970s, and the distribution systems for these stores are simpler and more direct. In many cases these stores have developed their own direct distribution systems that speed up the process. This is a growing pattern, but smaller retail outlets still cause the system to be complex, and it will remain so as long as they predominate.

Americans should not really try to penetrate the Japanese distribution system on their own. Instead, they should try to work closely with a Japanese agent or partner. Some successful Americans have hired a useful Japanese agent or company to promote their products. Other American businesses have done well by taking on a Japanese partner through a joint-venture agreement. For example, Coca-Cola of Japan has operated through a series of bottling partnerships with several Japanese concerns. Sears tackles the distribution system through its affiliation with Seibu Department Stores, Ltd., one of Japan's largest department store chains.

In a joint-venture or other form of partnership, it is important that both companies be compatible. The foreign company must adapt to market conditions and buyer preferences in Japan, and the Japanese company must not try to stifle the market by limiting the number of imports it will sell.

Efficiency of the Japanese Distribution System

A popular image of the Japanese distribution system is that of thousands of small neighborhood retailers who are accessible only after passing through several layers of middlemen, each adding an outrageous margin.[14] It isimportant to note that the actual number of middlemen depends upon the product and the individual company. For example, 57.6 percent of all fresh fish sold in Japan passes through three wholesalers before it reaches the retailer. On the other hand, about 90 percent of all shoes and furniture passes through only one wholesaler before reaching the retail outlet. Many of the larger goods companies in Japan have developed, over a long period of time, very short and efficient distribution channels. The leading companies in each product category tend to have greater market dominance as one moves away from urban areas. This is because these firms are financially stronger and better organized and because they have not been challenged by newer and smaller companies.

A Japanese company that is strong in one product area and introduces a new product often finds it difficult to establish distribution channels for the new product. An example is Ajinomoto, which has the major market share for monosodium glutamate. Although this food product can be found in almost every retail food shop in Japan, it is difficult to find Ajinomoto's mayonnaise, introduced over a decade ago, in any but the largest supermarkets and department stores.

A tactic often used to discourage market entry by foreign firms is to emphasize the large number of small retail outlets that "must be reached if you are to sell your products in this market." This, too, is a misconception, because the success and importance of the neighborhood retail outlet clearly depends upon offering a variety of products for sale. One can sell a product more effectively in large department stores. For example, many Japanese purchase clothing at department stores making them a primary outlet for this type of product. In contrast, in the late 1970s, about 120,000 stores in Japan sold beer and alcoholic beverages, making the small neighborhood store or vending machine run by a small store the primary outlets for these products. Even in the area of food products, growth in the number of Japanese superstores is causing a change in Japanese buying patterns. These outlets are being used more often by customers for purchases of processed food, although the neighborhood store is still the primary outlet for fresh meats, fruits, and vegetables. Liquor and fresh food products are also available in department stores, but their market share in this sector is very small.

After determining the relative importance of each type of retail outlet, a foreign firm entering the market must determine the importance of these outlets to the sale of the firm's products. For example, Japanese buy furniture primarily at specialty stores, including neighborhood stores, and department stores. However, most of these neighborhood specialty stores sell traditional Japanese furniture or cheaply and poorly constructed Western`style furniture. Western-style furniture of quality comparable to furniture that American and European suppliers might sell in Japan is sold primarily in department stores and in some large specialty stores.

An analysis of the distribution systems used by many of the U.S. consumer product firms selling in Japan reveals that the importance of the neighborhood outlet and the number of middlemen involved has been greatly exaggerated. The traditional distribution of several decades ago has been changing gradually to the advantage of foreign manufacturers. This has been due partly to the rise of superstores, formation and growth of chainstores, consolidation of many small wholesalers, and the efforts of Japanese manufacturers to establish direct and efficient distribution routes.

Japanese businessmen often respond to criticism of their distribution system by pointing out that it has taken Japanese companies years to develop their distribution channels and to earn the loyalty of wholesalers and retailers. These businessmen like to emphasize the aspects of feudal loyalty that exist in Japanese business, stating that business relations in Japan are not formed on the basis of profit alone. They claim that American businessmen who come rushing in with offers of a "better" deal will not often succeed because Japanese wholesalers and retailers demand more than a "good deal" in their business relations. In almost all phases of Japanese business activity, the question, "With whom is one dealing?" is as important as what is being discussed. For example, in deciding on whether to become an agent for an American company, a Japanese firm is just as interested in the American company's background and representatives as it is in the products the Americans are offering.

Japanese wholesalers and small retailers do impart a great amount of loyalty to their suppliers. The products the wholesaler receives from the manufacturer are his lifeblood. The primary wholesaler also knows that he is sustained by the loyalty of the people below him whether they be secondary wholesalers or retailers. He knows that they will continue to buy from him and will probably not abandon him in search of a better arrangement.

Trading Companies

Foreign businessmen involved with the Japanese or Chinese markets will come into contact with a unique institution, the Japanese trading company (*shosha*). They are unique organizations that play a vital role in foreign trade and provide the crucial link between foreign and domestic traders.

Japanese *shosha* are commercial enterprises specializing in foreign and domestic trade on behalf of their client companies. Trading companies are generally highly specialized concerns with a good understanding of many markets, market conditions and regulations, and economic conditions both in Japan and abroad. They play the key role of a middleman, linking individual companies with foreign and domestic markets and distributing commercial goods from one market to another. They also assist foreign firms in bringing their goods to Japan and often work as an intermediary between firms from two other nations.

The *shosha* date back to the first decade of the Meiji period (1868-1912) when the new Japanese government started to encourage Japanese companies to replace foreign firms that were then dominating Japanese trade. Trading companies were necessary in Japan then because of Japanese ignorance of foreign markets; Western lack of knowledge concerning Japanese customs, marketing and the Japanese distribution system; and the significant language barrier between Japan and foreign nations. Japanese trading companies rapidly developed the skills to meet these problems and became indispensible in Japan's commercial relations with foreign states.

Some of the more successful trading companies of the Meiji era grew into vast business combines before World War II. The combines (*zaibatsu*) were officially dissolved during the American Occupation of Japan (1945-52), but today many of the prewar companies continue to thrive as individual entities.

The Japanese government defines trading companies as commercial enterprises engaging both in wholesaling and in foreign trade. In recent years there have been three kinds of *shosha*: general trading companies (*sogo shosha*) handling a broad range of products from instant noodles to jet aircraft; smaller firms specializing in a special line or commodity; and the so-called "captive" companies owned by a manufacturer or retailer to serve its own corporate needs.

The *sogo shosha* differ from their far more numerous smaller rivals in several ways. The general trading companies are involved in both domestic and foreign trade, can handle a great diversity of goods, and are more able to provide both commercial and direct financing services for their customers. The smaller trading firms usually specialize only in foreign trade, handle a limited range of goods, and provide little or no financial services.

General trading companies (and, to a more limited extent, some smaller firms as well) perform a variety of services, including import and export sales, distribution of imported and domestic goods through channels they control, and forwarding and expediting. Through their close working ties with banks and other financial institutions and their access to capital, the general trading companies have long had a crucial function in the financing of the "hand-to-mouth" operations of many small suppliers, from whom they buy, and retailers, to whom they sell. The trading companies have performed another important economic role by their ability to pool business risks and to obtain lower rates in transportation and warehousing.

Each of the major *sogo shosha* maintains an extensive network of domestic offices that is closely linked to a wide overseas network. Managers of each of these branches in Japan and abroad have close contacts with local businessmen, government officials, and other community leaders. When opportunities arise for profitable business transactions, the manager will mobilize his corporate network to handle the deal. The trading company earns a commission for each transaction. Competition is so severe among the leading *sogo shosha* that the average profit margin was only nine-tenths of a percent of sales in the early 1980s. The emphasis is on volume of trade.

Roughly half of the business of the general trading companies is international. Most of this international business involves exports and imports to Japan, but a growing volume of trade consists of "third country trade" between two countries not involving Japan. The rest of their trade is domestic. In both foreign and domestic trade they arrange for shipping, insurance, delivery, inventory management, and other complex matters that need to be handled. Due to their huge size, the *sogo shosha* can achieve substantial savings in their performance of these matters.

The general trading companies can also work as "problem solvers" that arrange large-scale projects and deals by a consortia of firms. Thus, once when Kenya wanted to increase tourism by constructing a better and bigger airport, the Mitsubishi Corporation, through its affiliated trading company, put together a deal to build it. When Australia found that it had natural gas offshore that could be drilled, Mitsubishi organized a multimillion dollar project to drill and liquify the gas.

Mitsubishi, which buys over 25,000 different products ranging from grain to complex computers, is typical of the top ten *sogo shosha*. It had only about 800 employees, only a third of whom were Japanese, in its American offices in the early 1980s, but these offices generated well over $10 billion worth of trade transactions. Mitsubishi employees work in about 130 countries and its telex funnels several million words a day, providing the home office and branches with a wealth of information on such things as weather, labor disputes, interest rates, commodity prices, political crises, and technological advances. Indeed, the *sogo shosha* are "unparalleled by other companies, Japanese or foreign, in their international information network." Access to this information is crucial to their success.[15]

Leading General Trading Companies

Firm	Group Affiliation
Mitsubishi Corp.	Mitsubishi
Mitsui & Co.	Mitsui
C. Itoh & Co.	Dai-Ichi Kangyo Bank
Marubeni Corp.	Fuyo
Sumitomo Corp.	Sumitomo
Nissho-Iwai Company	Sanwa Bank
Toyo Menka Kaisha	Tokai Bank; Mitsui
Kanematsu-Gosho Lt.	Bank of Tokyo
Nichimen Company	Sanwa Bank

American companies wishing to do business with Japan would be well advised to contact the nearest office of a general trading company, since the *sogo shosha* have the experience and knowledge that Americans need to enter the Japanese market. Indeed, these companies act as masterful facilitators of commerce.

Future Prospects

Although Japan's trading companies showed no real signs of actual decline or decay in the late 1970s and early 1980s, their overall position in the rapidly expanding Japanese economy declined markedly after 1970. This decline is largely due to the types of products that they handle. Traditionally, these companies have focused their attention on the chemical and heavy industries -- like steel -- which have now entered a period of decline. The trading companies have played only a minimal role in the export of highly technical engineering machinery and components, automobiles, ships, industrial plants, and precision machinery. They also have little to do with the importation of petroleum.

By the early 1980s an increasing volume of trade was being handled directly by the manufacturers themselves, especially in the area of electronics and computers. Before 1960, the trading companies were responsible for over 80 percent of all imports and exports by value. By the late 1970s over 30 percent of trade was handled by the manufacturers themselves. This trend implies increasing competition among all trading firms as their share of the market dwindles.

CHAPTER VII - NOTES

1. *Business Week* (16 February 1987), p. 54.

2. *Ibid.*

3. *Ibid.*, p. 56.

4. Andrea Boltho, *Japan: an Economic Survey* (London: Oxford University Press, 1974), p. 141.

5. W. V. Rapp and R. A. Feldman, "Japan's Economic Strategy and Prospects" in W. J. Barnds, *Japan and the United States: Challenges and Opportunities* (New York: New York University Press, 1979), p. 118.

6. *Ibid.*, p. 102.

7. Boltho, pp. 154-56.

8. L. B. Krause and Sueo Sekiguchi, "Japan and the World Economy," in Hugh Patrick and Henry Rosovsky, pp. 440-450.

9. *Ibid.*, p. 445. Note: Readers interested in obtaining more information about foreign investment in Japan should consult the Krause-Sekiguchi article and Dan Fenno Henderson's book, *Foreign Enterprise in Japan: Laws and Policies* (Rutland, VT: Tuttle, 1975).

10. Regional offices of the Department of Commerce usually have an agent familiar with Japan and a series of booklets that are extremely useful. Another useful resource is the Japan Economic Institute of America, 1000 Connecticut Avenue, NW, Washington, DC. The JEI is funded by and works on behalf of the Japanese government. Its aim is to work with Americans interested in doing business in Japan. One may also seek advice from Japanese trading companies. Most of the data for this chapter was gathered at the Boston office of the Department of Commerce in the early 1980s and from various USDC booklets, especially *Japan: A Growth Market for U.S. Consumer Products* (1978 edition). Readers are urged to make good use of these booklets.

11. Americans interested in marketing in Japan should see the brief film, "The Colonel Comes to Japan." It is an excellent analysis of Kentucky Fried Chicken's successful move into Japan in the 1970s and early 1980s.

12. When I was living in Japan in the late 1970s, I would wash my family's clothes in a tiny coin-operated laundromat. The washing machines and dryers were much smaller than their American counterparts, but worked just as well. The owner was doing very well until he ordered a huge washing machine from the United States. The American machine worked very well; it

had two to three times the capacity of the Sanyo machines in the laundromat and it cost only 150 yen to operate it as opposed to 100 yen one paid for to operate the smaller Japanese models. I used the American machine with great zeal, but unfortunately, few if any Japanese dared to put their clothes in it. The manager told me that his customers complained that the machine was too big and made too much noise. They were reluctant to even try it out.

13. The manager of my local laundry in Tokyo was a typical small wholesaler. The laundromat occupied one small room on the bottom floor of a small two-floorhouse. The other room below was full of Coke and Fanta cartons, about half of which were full at any time. Two or three times a week a small truck would pull up to deliver new bottles and to take away empty cartons. Several times a day the laundromat owner would put a few bottles on the back of his motorcycle and take them to local shops.

14. This section is developed from the United States Department of Commerce's 1978 brochure, *Japan: A Growth Market for US Consumer Products*, pp. 16-17.

15. Ezra Vogel, *Japan as Number One* (Cambridge: Harvard University Press, 1979), p. 44.

CHAPTER VIII

TECHNOLOGY AND THE FUTURE

Japan's miraculous growth after World War II was due primarily to the development of a sound industrial base. The maturation of its automobile and steel industries was symbolic of a nation whose economic well-being was largely based on heavy industries. These industries continue today, but they do not offer much in the way of future growth and profits. Rather, it is in the area of "high tech" that Japan will emerge as the standard bearer of the 21st century.

Japanese companies substantially increased their world market share in the early and mid-1980s in such areas as computers, telecommunications, fiber optics, biotechnology, and other related fields. The Japanese were successful enough in their research efforts to close the technology gap between them and the United States. Ezra Vogel asserts that Japan's greater supply of new engineers, especially electrical engineers, enabled it to expand its lead in product engineering and to move quickly to computer-aided manufacturing.[1]

Japan in recent years has taken the lead in consumer electronics, applied robotics and other forms of factory automation, photographic equipment, random access memory chips, and supercomputers. Its successes in these fields will probably lead to continued rapid economic growth through the 1990s despite declines in the traditional manufacturing sector. As Japan's computer, telecommunications, semiconductor, robotics and related industries grow, they will carry the nation's economy along with them. Indeed, by the early 1980s Japan reached the point where these industries for the first time had a higher export value than that of Japanese automobiles. The new technologies are already beginning to reinvigorate the Japanese economy that by 1987 had begun to show some signs of sluggishness and decay.

The secret to the new burst of high growth in the electronics and information-related industries is, of course, productivity. For example, integrated circuit memory costs are falling steadily at a rate exceeding 30 per cent a year, and each price reduction has made the technology available for many new uses.   Thus, such new products as personal computers and videotape recorders were born, and new industries, like personal computer software, have emerged.[2] The profit surge in these fields will be important to Japan's future economic growth.

As noted earlier, it appears that Japan will lead the United States by a growing margin in extracting economic gain from microelectronics technology.   The Japanese have concentrated on a wide range of commercially attractive technologies, while American researchers have to a great extent devoted much of their research to military or defense projects that are of little monetary value.   The research devoted to President Reagan's "Star Wars" program is a good case in point.   According to one American observer, "Many such projects have been commissioned by the U.S. Department of Defense, which clearly lacks the Midas touch: every year it turns $300 billion into objects of no economic value."[3]

There are other examples of this problem.   While American researchers went ahead to produce an elegant and technically advanced 64K RAM chip, Japanese technicians put together a workable, less expensive product and grabbed the lion's share of the world market from the United States.   Similarly, while the United States has made some very complex, expensive, and interesting robots, Japan is far ahead in making robots that are suited for work.

A new period of economic growth will emerge from the advances of the Japanese in these fields, and this renewed growth will have global implications due to the huge size of the Japanese economy.   Japan's first economic miracle literally ran out of fuel as its automobile and other oil-dependent mechanical devices found it difficult to withstand large oil price increases.   The second postwar industrial revolution is being powered by microelectronics, which require very little in the way of natural resources.   Japan will lead the world with slowly increasing GNP growth rates which will continue to rise as technology advances.

The Importance of Technology

A symbol of modern Japan is the high level of technology one finds everywhere in everyday life. There is the popular notion that Japan is a nation of copiers, that the Japanese make up for their own lack of originality by improving upon the ideas of others. The truth is that much of the fruit of research and development in high tech in recent years has been born of Japanese scientists and researchers and that much of Japan's postwar economic success is due to the ability of the Japanese to market their technology to the world.[4]

Japan is a nation lacking natural resources, especially oil. This weakness may have actually worked in Japan's favor in the early postwar era. Since there were no domestic resource industries, there was no need to worry about protecting domestic companies, and Japan was able to secure for itself the cheapest resources from around the world. Unfortunately, rural resources, such as oil, are growing scarcer and more expensive.

Japan's industrial and technological power constantly gives birth to new products, which in turn has made the nation's growth and development possible. Japan has the ability to produce good products cheaply and in quantity. In this sense Japan is not a resource-poor country. Growth will continue because Japanese industry is pouring its full energy into research and development on the major products of the decade.[5] Many of the "high-tech" electronic goods that the Japanese are promoting in the mid-1980s include the following:

> - Office computers, personal computers, high performance terminals, other automated office machines, fiber-optics systems.
> - Industrial robots, sophisticated numerically controlled machine tools, computer-aided design/computer-aided manufacturing systems, flexible manufacturing systems.
> - Very large-scale integrated circuits, new semi-conductor elements, carbon fibers, amorphous semi-conductors and other new materials.
> - Videodiscs and players, solid-state video cameras with built-in videotape recorders, electronic musical instruments.[6]

All of these products are being commercialized, and technological work on them all is making very good progress. There are some areas where the Japanese continue to lag behind the United States (such as in defense, space, and aircraft technology) and some others where the Japanese hold a distinct lead, but overall the Americans and Japanese are about even in technological development. The Japanese, however, make a specialty of mass production and since many of the items listed above are mass produced, it is probable that Japan will find itself in a superior position regarding performance and price as these products reach the commercial stage.

Japan's Technological Position

It is difficult to measure Japan's technological position in the late 1980s because there is tremendous variation across the sectors. Japan has reached state-of-the-art technology in a variety of areas: iron and steel production, agricultural chemicals, new materials, nuclear energy processing, semiconductors, computer peripherals, office automation, robotics, flexible manufacturing systems, certain areas of telecommunications, pharmaceuticals, biotechnology, and industrial lasers.[7]

Japan has done well in areas where the theoretical parameters surrounding these technologies are well known, the technological trajectories are predictable, and product advances are made in continuous or incremental steps. Progress in Japan has been much slower in technologies where the theoretical parameters for problem solving are highly complex (e.g., jet aircraft design) and technological trajectories are not readily predictable (e.g., advanced software). Japanese firms are not as apt to make seminal inventions that lead to the creation of whole new industries, due in part to the relatively low level of government research and development (R&D) and to the narrowly applied nature of much of commercial R&D.[8]

In the early 1980s Japan lagged far behind the United States in various military technologies including the following: aerospace, jet aircraft, avionics, computer-aided design and computer-aided manufacturing, and security-related information processing. Japan fares far better in certain dual-purpose technologies with both military and civilian applications where commercial markets are large and barriers to entry are not that imposing. For example, Japan has made great strides in space research in recent years and was the third nation after the U.S. and USSR to launch a satellite.

The Pursuit of Knowledge and Information

Ezra Vogel in his book, *Japan as Number One*, notes:

> If any single factor explains Japanese success, it is the group-oriented quest for knowledge. In virtually every important organization and community where people share a common interest, from the national government to individual private firms, from cities to villages, devoted leaders worry about the future of their organizations, and to these leaders, nothing is more important than the information and knowledge that the organizations might one day need. When Daniel Bell, Peter Drucker, and others hailed the coming of the postindustrial society in which knowledge replaced capital as society's most important resource, this new conception became a great rage in Japan's leading circles.
>
> But these leading circles were merely articulating the latest formation of what had already become conventional Japanese wisdom, the supreme importance of the pursuit of knowledge.[9]

Japan is rapidly becoming a post-industrial nation whose future wealth and well-being depend largely upon the accumulation and use of information, knowledge, and intelligence. Tom Stonier, a British scientist, notes that the rising unemployment in Western nations since the 1970s reflects a fundamental structural change in their societies because of another ongoing shift -- to the post-industrial economy in which information can generate wealth.[10]

In the 1970s, Daniel Bell, a Harvard sociologist, presented the outlines for what he called the post-industrial society. What Bell calls the "axial principle" of this post-industrial society is the centrality and codification of theoretical knowledge. One finds along that axis a new kind of intellectual technology, the spread of a knowledge class, the switch from goods to services, and a change in the character of work. In Japan, the new intellectual technology is artificial intelligence -- machines that amplify human thought.[11]

The result is a national effort to develop the new "Fifth Generation" of computers which will have reasoning powers and which will be self-programming. In 1982 a research and development program, called the Institute for New Generation Computer Technology (ICOT), was started with initial funding and new laboratories provided by the Japanese government.[12]

The goal of the Japanese is to do the following:

> Develop computers for the 1990s and beyond --
> intelligent computers that will be able to converse with humans
> in natural language and understand speech and pictures.
> These will be computers that can learn, associate, make
> inferences, make decisions, and otherwise behave in ways we
> have always considered the exclusive province of human
> reason.[13]

If, in fact, such machines can be developed by the 1990s, they will lead to a revolution in productivity in the work force. They will also enhance the quality of manufactured goods that Japan will produce because of knowledge that will be brought to bear on their design and manufacture.

It is not yet certain how successful the Japanese will be in this endeavor. Some critics have noted that artificial intelligence was not a promising line of inquiry, but research has continued with promising results throughout the mid-1980s.

Japan and its Future Role as a Major "High-Tech" Power

Earlier it was noted that Tokyo is rapidly becoming the world's major financial center and Ezra Vogel states that:

> With the world's best-educated work force, with the
> world's trading companies collecting the information, with the
> world's best informed bureaucrats leading the government, and
> with the rapid application of the world's most up-to-date
> technology, they (Japanese leaders) are increasingly optimistic
> about their ability to make Tokyo the information capital of
> the world.[14]

Japan would indeed become Number One in many critical areas from which it would gain immense economic wealth and power. There are other areas, however, where Japan would remain very weak. Japan will continue as a military and political weakling when compared to the superpowers, and it is weak in several key areas of research, including the natural sciences. Moreover, World War II has not faded in the memories of Japan's Asian neighbors. The image of Japan as a selfish and rather dangerous imperialist power is not uncommon in the newspapers of South Korea, China, the Philippines and other Asian states with ties to Japan.

Japan must work to avert its superior and haughty attitudes of the past. Above all, it must avoid the temptation to arm itself. A turn to rearmament and military strength would divert a lot of money and energy into a nonproductive part of the economy and, more importantly, might make some of its neighbors nervous or frightened over even the vaguest hint of a return to the militarism of the past.

Japan's relationship with the United States is also of utmost importance. The U.S. is Japan's leading market for exports and for foreign investment. The Japanese must make every endeavor to keep American markets open for their products even at the expense of opening up some more of their doors to U.S. goods. The defense treaty between the Japanese and the United States is beneficial to both sides. Japan exchanges American access to its ports and several military bases for an American nuclear "umbrella" that supposedly protects Japan from outside military attack. Thus, it is critical that the Japanese work to moderate the flow of their goods into the United States and that they continue to invest extensively throughout the United States.

Japan must learn to behave as a responsible power by removing its unfortunate arrogant tendencies of the past. It must be sensitive to the needs and complaints of its neighbors, work harder to share its wealth and know-how, and should be more open to imports and foreign investment. Two generations ago a powerful but equally vulnerable Japan chose a lonesome and isolated path that eventually led to national ruin. A more open and conciliatory approach to the outside world and a more cooperative attitude in the long run will enable Japan to retain its position at the top of the pack.

CHAPTER VIII - NOTES

1.   Ezra Vogel, *Comeback: Case by Case -- Building the Resurgence of American Business* (Tokyo: Tuttle, 1985), p. 18.

2.   Christopher Mead, "Second Japanese Miracle on the Horizon," *Creative Computing* (August 1984), p. 120.

3.   *Ibid.*, p. 123.

4.   *Ibid.*

5.   Masanori Moritani, *Japanese Technology: Getting the Best for the Least* (Tokyo: Simul Press, 1982), p. 213.

6.   *Ibid.*

7.   Daniel I. Okimoto and Gary Saxonhouse, "Technology and the Future of the Economy," in Yamamura and Yasuba, *The Political Economy of Japan*, p. 396.

8.   *Ibid.*, pp. 396-399.

9.   Ezra Vogel, *Japan as Number One*, p. 27.

10.   Tom Stonier, *The Wealth of Information* (London: 1983).

11.   Edward Feigenbaum and Pamela McCorduck, "The Fifth Generation: Japan's Computer Challenge to the World," in *Creative Computing* (August 1984), p. 105.

12.   *Ibid.*, p. 104.

13.   *Ibid.*, p. 104.

14.   Vogel, *Comeback*, p. 167.

SOURCE MATERIAL

INTERVIEWS

Interviews were conducted on the dates indicated. In some cases additional meetings were held, but only the date of the initial interview has been given.

Matsuoka Osamu
Managing Editor, Seikyo Shimbun
6/12/84

Mihara Asahiko
Member of the Diet
8/16/87

Nakano Hideki
Manager, KDD
8/19/85

Shimada Yukio
Professor of International Law, Waseda University
8/18/85

Sone Yuko
IBM Japan
3/29/86

Tsukamoto Akira
Journalist for Nippon Television
8/20/85

BIBLIOGRAPHY

Abegglen, James C. and Stalk, George, Jr. *Kaisha: The Japanese Corporation*. (New York: Basic Books, Inc., 1985).

Applied Research Corporation Technology Transfer Institute. *(Learning from the Japanese Experience*. Singapore: Maruzen Asia, 1982).

Asahi Nenkan 1986. (Tokyo: Asahi Shimbunsha, 1986.)

Asahi Shimbun. (1986-1987).

Barnds, W. J., Ed. *Japan and the United States: Challenges and Opportunities*. (New York: New York University Press, 1979).

Blaker, Michael. *Japanese International Negotiating Style*. (New York: Columbia University Press, 1977).
Boltho, Andrea. *Japan: An Economic Survey*. (London: Oxford University Press, 1974).

Burks, Ardath W. *Japan: Portrait of a Post industrial Power.* (Boulder: Westview Press, 1981).

Burstein, Daniel. "Rising Sun on Wall Street," *New York Magazine*, March 2, 1987.

Business Week. 1986-88.

Susan Chira, "A Job Crunch Jolts Japan." *The New York Times*, January 18, 1987.

Clark, Rodney. *The Japanese Company.* (New Haven: Yale University Press, 1979).

Darman, Richard G. "What's Wrong with Japan Bashing." *U.S. News & World Report*, October 5, 1987.

De Mente, Boye. *The Japanese Way of Doing Business.* (Englewood, NJ: Prentice Hall, 1981).

Deutsch, Michael F. *Doing Business with the Japanese.* (New York: Mentor, 1985).

Dreyfus, Joel. "Fear and Trembling in the Colossus," in *Fortune International*, 30 March 1987, p. 32.

The Economist, 25 October, 1986.

Ellington, Lucien and Rice, Richard, ed. "Intercultural Contact: The Japanese in Rutherford County, Tennessee," *The Occasional Papers of the Virginia Consortium for Asian Studies.* IV (Spring, 1987), pp. 26-34.

Feigenbaum, Edward and McCorduck, Pamela. "The Fifth Generation: Japan's Computer Challenge to the World." *Creative Computing*, August, 1984.

Fiske, Edward B. "Japanese Education Fades at the Finish," in *The New York Times*: Sec. 4, p. 6. January 11, 1987.

Frank, Isaiah, Ed. *The Japanese Economy in International Perspective.* (Baltimore: The Johns Hopkins Press, 1975).

Gibney, Frank. *Miracle by Design: The Real Reasons Behind Japan's Economic Success.* (New York: Times Books, 1982).

Guest, James. "Doing Business in Japan," *Vermont Affairs.* III (Summer, 1987), 3-7.

Haitani, Kanji. *The Japanese Economic System.* (Lexington: Lexington Books, 1976).

Halloran, Richard. *Japan: Images and Realities.* (New York: Random House, 1969).

Harvard Business Review, Ed., *How Japan Works.* (Cambridge: Harvard University Press, 1981).

Henderson, Dan Fenno. *Foreign Enterprise in Japan.* (Rutland: Tuttle, 1975).

Hirschmeier, J. and Yui, T. *The Development of Japanese Business: 1600-1980.* (London: George Allen & Unwin, 1981).

Ho, Alfred K. *Japan's Trade Liberalization in the 1960s.* (White Plains, N.Y.: International Arts and Sciences Press, Inc., 1973).

Hofheinz, Roy Jr. and Calder, Kent E. *The Eastasia Edge.* (New York: Basic Books, Inc., 1982).

Ishizuka, Masahiko. "The Real Cause of the U.S. - Japan Trade Defecit," *Nihon Keizai Shimbun,* January 17, 1987.

Japan Center for International Exchange, The Silent Power: Japan's Identity and World Role. Tokyo: Simul Press, 1976.

Japan Economic Survey. 1985-88.

The Japan Economic Institute of America, *U.S.-Japan Economic Relations Yearbook 1984-1985.* (Washington: JEI, 1986).

The Japan Times Weekly. 1986-88.

Johnson, Chalmers. *MITI and the Japanese Miracle: The Growth of Industrial Policy, 1925-1975.* (Stanford: Stanford University Press, 1982).

Satoshi Kamata, *Japan in the Passing Lane. An Insider's Account of Life in a Japanese Auto Factory.* (New York: Pantheon Books, 1982).

Kaplan, M., Ed. *Japan, America, and the Future World Order.* (New York: Heath, 1976).

Korea Herald. 1987-88.

Lockwood, William W., ed. *The State and Enterprise in Modern Japan.* (Princeton: Princeton University Press, 1965).

Magaziner, Ira C. and Hout, Thomas M. *Japanese Industrial Policy.* (Berkeley: Institute of International Studies, University of California, 1980).

Mead, Christopher. "Second Japanese Miracle on the Horizon." *Creative Computing,* August 1984.

Mitsubishi Bank Review, January, 1987.

Michio Morishima, *Why Japan Succeeded.* (Cambridge: Cambridge University Press, 1982).

Akio Morita. *Made in Japan.* (New York: Dutton, 1986).

Moritani, Masanori. *Japanese Technology: Getting the Best for the Least.* (Tokyo: Simul Press, 1982).

Mushakoji Kinhide, "Nihon bunka to Nihon gaiko," [Japanese Culture and Japanese Foreign Policy] in Mushakoji, Ed., *Kokusai seiji to Nihon* [*International Politics and Japan*], (Tokyo, 1967).

Takafusa Nakamura, *The Postwar Japanese Economy: Its Development and Structure.* (Tokyo: Tokyo University Press, 1980).

NBC News, *White Paper on Japan.* Broadcast 4 May 1987.

Norbury, Paul and Bownas, Geoffrey, Ed., *Business in Japan: A Guide to Japanese Business Practice and Procedure.* (Boulder, Colorado: Westview Press, 1980).

William Ouchi, *Theory Z.* (New York, Avon Books, 1980).

Patrick, Hugh, and Rosovsky, Henry, eds., *Asia's New Giant: How the Japanese Economy Works.* (Washington, D.C.: Brookings Institution, 1976).

Pempel, T. J. *Japan: The Dilemmas of Success.* (New York: Foreign Policy Association, 1986).

Pye, Lucien W. *Asian Power and Politics: The Cultural Dimensions of Authority.* (Cambridge: Harvard University Press, 1985).

Reischauer, Edwin. The Japanese. (Cambridge: Harvard University Press, 1977).

Rosenberger, Nancy. "Japanese Women: Paradoxes of Power and Self." Unpublished paper presented at the annual meeting of the Southeast Conference of the Association for Asian Studies at Chatanooga, Tennessee, 16 January 1987.

Sakiya, Tetsuo. *Honda Motor: The Men, The Management, The Machines.* (Tokyo: Kodansha Int, Ltd., 1982).

Sanders, Sol. *Honda: The Man and his Machines.* (Tokyo: Tuttle, 1977).

Shinohara Miyohei, *Industrial Growth, Trade, and Dynamic Patterns in the Japanese Economy.* (Tokyo: Tokyo University Press, 1982).

Snowden, Sondra. "How to Negotiate with the Japanese," in *U.S. News & World Report*, September 28, 1987.

Stoever, William A. *Renegotiations in International Business Transactions.* (Lexington, MA.: Lexington Books, 1981.

Time (Asian Edition). 1986-87.

"Timid Investors -- Japanese Institutional Investors," *Tokyo Business Today*, August, 1987.

Vogel, Ezra. Combeback. *Case By Case: Building the Resurgence of American Business.* (Tokyo: Tuttle, 1985).

_____. *Japan as Number One.* (Cambridge: Harvard University Press, 1979).

_____. Ed. *Modern Japanese Organization and Decision Making.* (Berkeley: University of California Press, 1975).

Washington Post, 22 June 1986.

"Japan's Unemployment Problem," in *The Wall Street Journal*, 6 November 1986, p. 1.

Wall Street Journal, 6 November 1986.

Washington Post, 20 September 1987.

Woronoff, Jon. *Inside Japan Inc.* (Tokyo: Lotus Books, 1983).

_____. *Japan's Commercial Empire.* (Tokyo: Lotus Books, 1984).

Yamamura, Kozo and Yasuba Yasukichi, Ed., *The Political Economy of Japan: The Domestic Transformation.* (Stanford: Stanford University Press, 1987).

Michael Y. Yoshino, "Japanese Management," in *The Encyclopedia of Japan.* (Tokyo: Kodansha, 1983).

Young, Alexander K. *The Sogo Shosha: Japan's Multinational Trading Companies.* (Boulder, Colorado: Westview Press, 1979).

INDEX

Abegglen, James C., 9
Administrative Guidance, 94-951
Agent-Pricing Problems, 138-139
amae, 33-34
American written constitution of Japan, 16
Americans, working with Japanese, 39-47
awase ("consensus") culture, 41-42

Bank of Japan, 84
Bankers, role of, 80-81
Bureaucracy, 86
Business cards,

China, influence on Japanese culture 3-5
Communication with Japanese, 31-49
Companies, role in economic development, 13-27
Computers, 155-160
Confucianism, 86-89
         Confucian tradition in Japan, 4-5
Conservative parties, 15
Consumers in Japan, 129-130
Contracts, 45-47

Decision-making, 61-62
Department Stores, 142-143
Distribution system in Japan, 144-148

Economic development, 7-9
Economic Planning Agency, 84
Education, 52-53
         in Meiji period, 5-6
         post-war 8
Electronics industry, 80-81
endaka, 78
Enryo, 34
erabi ("choice") culture, 41-42

Fair Trade Commission, 97
Farming, 70-72
Foreign investment in Japan, 133-134
Foreign Trade, viii, 132-133

Geography, 2-3
Gephardt Amendment, vii-viii
Gephardt, Congressman Richard, vii
Godfather Concept, 63
Government and business, 83-98

Group structure, 36-39
Guest, James, 121-122
Hawley-Smoot Act, viii
Hawley, Willis C., viii
Honda Corporation, 22-24
Honda Soichiro, 22-24
Housing, 21-22

Industrial policy, 91-95

Japanese language, 31-33
Japanese personality, 33-36
"Japan-bashing," 122-124
"Japan-Inc.," 83, 141

Keidanren, 97
Kentucky Fried Chicken in Japan, 13
Kunin, Madeline, 121

Land, price of, 20-21
Liberal-Democratic Party, 15, 85, 20,
Lifetime Employment, 53-55
Living Standards, 19-21

MacArthur, General, 103
Management, 51-65
          Executive style, 60-61
          women in, 58-60
Managers (Japanese) in the U.S., 64-65
Marketing agent, 136-138
Marketing in Japan, 134-135
Ministry of Agriculture, 86
Ministry of Finance, 83, 92-95
Ministry of International Trade and Industry, 84,
                              92-96
MITI, See Ministry of International Trade and Industry
Mitsubishi Heavy Industries, 77
Morita, Akio 24-27

Natural resources, 7
Negotiations, 41-47
Neighborhood stores, 144

Occupational Structure, 69-81
          primary sector, 70-72
          secondary sector, 72-78
          tertiary sector, 78-81
Ohmae, Kenichi, 18-20

Personality, 33-36

Political system of Japan, 89-91
Population, 2
Reischauer, Edwin, 83
Resources, 2-3
Retailing in Japan, 142
Retirement, 56-57
ringisho, 62

Salary, 56-57
Savings, 12
Self-Defense forces, 16
Seniority System, 55-57
Shinyo, 40
Shipping, 76
Sony Corporation, 24-27
Specialty stores, 143
Stalk, George, 9
Steel industry, 75, 77
Supermarkets, 143-144
Superstores, 143

Taxation, 84
Technology, 155-161
Tennessee, Japanese investment in, 117-120
Trademark Law, Japan, 138
Trading Companies, 139-142
        General trading companies, 139
Traditional Restrictive Practices, 138

Unemployment, 75, 77
Unions, 58
United States and Japan, 101-103, 104-109
        Japanese investment in U.S., 110-115
        Japanese ownership of companies in the U.S., 115-
        120
        Public opinion, 105-106
        Trade problems, 103-104, 108-110

Vermont, Japanese investment in, 120-122
Vogel, Ezra, 85

Wages, 56-57, 129-130
Women, 14, 58-60
Work habits 8, 14, 17
Woronof, Jon, 16

zaibatsu, 149

MELLEN STUDIES IN BUSINESS

1. Khalid R. Mehtabin, **Comparative Management**
2. Donald G. Jones and Patricia I. Bennett (eds.), **A Bibliography of Business Ethics**
3. Giichi Sugimoto, translated by William Cook, **Six-Sided Management: Righteousness, Gratitude, Compassion**
4. Alexander J. Matejko, **A Christian Approach To Work and Industry**